T0317590

The Mental Strategies of Top Traders

The Mental Strategies of Top Traders

The Psychological Determinants of Trading Success

ARI KIEV

WILEY

John Wiley & Sons, Inc.

Published by John Wiley & Sons, Inc., Hoboken, New Jersey.
Published simultaneously in Canada.

For general information on our other products and services or for technical support, please contact our Customer Care Department within the United States at (800) 762-2974, outside the United States at (317) 572-3993 or fax (317) 572-4002.

Wiley also publishes its books in a variety of electronic formats. Some content that appears in print may not be available in electronic books. For more information about Wiley products, visit our website at www.wiley.com.

Library of Congress Cataloging-in-Publication Data:

Kiev, Ari.
  The mental strategies of top traders : the psychological determinants of trading success / Ari Kiev.
     p.   cm. — (Wiley trading series)
  Includes index.
  ISBN 978-0-470-50953-1 (cloth)
  1. Investments—Psychological aspects.   2. Stocks—Psychological aspects.
3. Speculation—Psychological aspects.   4. Investments—Case studies.   I. Title.
  HG4515.15.K542   2010
  332.6401'9–dc22

                                                                    2009021669

Printed in the United States of America

10 9 8 7 6 5 4 3 2 1

For Phyllis, with all my love

Contents

Acknowledgments   xi

Introduction   1

CHAPTER 1   Intellect, Instinct, and Guts:
            Understanding the Psychological
            Profile   7

A History of Success   14
The Ability to Take Risk   15
Creativity and Originality   16
Self-Awareness, Self-Control, and Resilience   17
    Teaching Traders Self-Assessment and Self-Control   18
Teamwork and Leadership   19
Putting It All Together   21
Case Study on Finding the Right Candidate   21
    Job Requirements   21
    Potential Candidates   22
    The Bottom Line   25
The Perfect Candidate?   26
Chapter in Review   27

CHAPTER 2   Planning for Action: The Importance
            of Goal-Directedness   29

Making a Plan   30
Case Study on Setting a Goal   31
Case Study on Having a Variant Perception   35

Personality Factors and Goal-Setting   **42**
Recognizing Goal-Directed Individuals   **44**
Case Study on Recognizing Goal-Directedness   **47**
    Fred's Strengths: The Three *Cs*   47
    Fred's Weaknesses: The Three *Is*   48
Goal-Directedness in Turbulent Times   **50**
    Own Your Stuff   51
    Review the Game Films   51
    Switch Gears?   52
    Be Realistic   52
    Stay True to Your Strengths   52
    Maintain Focus   53
Chapter in Review   **54**

**CHAPTER 3 "Fire in the Belly": The Ability
to Take Appropriate Risk**   **57**

A Picture of Successful Risk Management   **57**
    Trading Philosophy   59
    Handling Drawdowns   59
    Head versus Heart   60
    Reviewing Risk Statistics   60
    Examining Personality Factors   63
Learning to Upgrade Your Performance   **71**
Chapter in Review   **77**

**CHAPTER 4 Thinking Outside the Box:
The Importance of Ingenuity**   **79**

Case Study on the Satisfaction of Creative Thinking   **80**
The Strategic Thinker   **81**
Case Study on Learning to Be Creative   **82**
Idea Construction   **88**
Developing a Variant Perception   **88**
Case Study on Creative Thinking   **89**
    Idea Evaluation Checklist   92
Defining Expectational Analysis   **94**

Case Study on Knowing the Business 95
Case Study on Expectational Analysis 100
  Raising Your Conviction 103
Idea Velocity 105
Idea Timing 105
Idea Completion 106
The Psychological Dimension 109
Case Study on Communicating Effectively 111
Chapter in Review 114

CHAPTER 5 Separating Emotions and Decisions: The Ability to Be Self-Aware 117

Case Study on the Emotion of Drawdowns 118
The Source of Fear 121
Case Study on Trading Stress 123
Self-Esteem and Self-Discipline 125
Learning from Drawdowns 128
Case Study on Self-Assessing During Drawdowns 129
Getting Comfortable with the Uncomfortable 131
Case Study on Being Comfortable with Discomfort 132
  Teaching Traders Self-Assessment and Self-Control 136
Managing Stress Well 136
Chapter in Review 140

CHAPTER 6 Nurturing Team Players: Listening, Learning, and Working Together 143

Characteristics of a Team Player 144
  Responsible 144
  Positive and Encouraging 145
  Competitive 148
  Coachable 149
Finding Complements to Your Team 151
Case Study on a Comparison of Traders 153
The Importance of Communication 155
Chapter in Review 159

CHAPTER 7   Leadership: Directing Success   161

Empowering a Culture of Change   162
Case Study on Creating a Culture of Change   162
Encouraging Responsibility   171
Case Study on the Challenges of Responsibility   173
Exploring Potential Leaders   176
Case Studies on Finding Potential Leaders   177
Endeavoring for Success   183
Case Study on a Failure to Lead   184
Chapter in Review   189

Index   191

Acknowledgments

Many people have helped me with this book. I am especially grateful to the hedge fund managers who have provided me with the opportunity to explore the interface between trading and psychology. I want to thank Tricia Brown for helping me organize many hours of interviews with traders and for her efforts in helping me to edit several versions of the original manuscript. As in the past, much of this would not have been done without the support of my beloved wife, who has always been there to encourage me to stay focused on the project through the many stages of its progress.

Introduction

From my perspective, investing is not simply a fair coin-toss where everyone has the same chance of winning or losing. There is no question that some people consistently outperform other players. So, the question becomes, "How can you increase your chances of winning?" That question is the driving force behind this book. While I cannot define a step-by-step formula for trading success, I have outlined various attributes of successful traders in the hope that by learning more about them you can improve your own odds and the odds of those around you.

Certain psychological characteristics of successful people obviously can be found in successful traders* and portfolio managers. However, there is something unique about investing that requires some additional, seemingly incongruent, characteristics. For example, the most successful investors will have a high tolerance for *risk-taking* in a *controlled* way. They will also have a capacity for making rapid decisions with *insufficient information* but with *sufficient thoroughness* and discernment to increase the probability of success. They will have a *strong desire for wins* but have a *tolerance for losses*. They will know how to recover from failure and to persevere because at least 40 to 50 percent of their trades are going to be wrong.

Of course, I have explored many of these themes in my earlier books. In *Trading to Win*, I discussed the commitment to win as opposed to trading to avoid losing. *Trading in the Zone* tackled the issue of how an individual can get outside his own skin and function in an objective way, zone-focused and intensely concentrated on the present moment in the context of a longer-term objective. *The Psychology of Risk* addressed overcoming fears and inhibitions about the possibility of losing, and *Hedge Fund*

---

*I consider the terms *PM* and *trader* completely equivalent; therefore throughout the course of this manuscript I will use them interchangeably.

Masters specifically tackled the issue of anxiety. *Leadership* offered readers information on how to empower others in line with these same issues. Each of these books has dealt with another dimension of the personality of the successful trader. So, what makes this book different?

The Mental Strategies of Top Traders attempts to take another cut at the issue of successful trading by looking across a range of skill sets that are component parts of the successful trader, including among other things a goal-oriented strategy, risk management, creative thinking, and a capacity for collaboration and leadership. What is the nature of investing and trading in terms of being a probabilistic field of endeavor, and what kinds of traits and personality characteristics must be developed to increase the likelihood of success?

First, the stock market *is* a probabilistic field providing various outcomes. The successful investor must be psychologically geared toward correctly handicapping the odds so as to increase his chances of winning in a continuously changing paradigm. Approaching the markets this way flies in the face of most academic approaches to the markets, which are predicated on the notion that the markets are efficient and that consistent winning by an investor is probably more likely due to luck than to skill.

My view is that the field of investing is like sports betting and that you as a trader can increase your odds of winning by learning to bet on high-probability bets. Indeed, with some training and practice, you can develop your ability to handicap the probabilities in order to be able to do so. Where there are a variety of probable approaches, there are a few that have very favorable odds, and the trader's edge is to find those few and rare high-probability bets, do the work to build conviction, and then press the bet, holding the bet even after portions of your datapoints have been realized and the price of a stock has moved up. In effect, it is possible to build on already-existing personality strengths so as to develop the ability to function in a goal-oriented way, and learn to cut losses and maximize winning bets. It is also possible, as we shall see later in this book, to begin to look at company-specific and sector-specific data in your analysis of companies so as to get comfortable in making nonconsensus, high-risk, and high-probability bets—the ones where there is the greatest gap between current and future expectations of price.

Unlike the situation at the racetrack or in other types of sports betting where the odds are posted, they are not posted in the marketplace. As an investor, you have to learn to read the odds by figuring out the expectations that are built into present prices—specifically what expectations are built into current data about a company that have not yet been fully expressed in the price of the stock, or finding mispricings where the full value of the stock has not been fully expressed in the present price but will be over time as certain events unfold. This is not where the vast majority of traders spend their time or where the sell-side research focuses its published reports, but it is where you will have to invest a lot of your research efforts if you are to uncover expected value.

More often than not, investors look at the fundamentals of a company as the source of the price, failing to differentiate fundamentals from the expectations implied by the price of the stock. Investors will often buy a stock based on strong fundamentals even if expectations are not positive. They may also avoid buying a stock with weak fundamentals even when expectations for increased prices are present. As a result, most investors fail to adequately calculate the odds of positive or negative stock price movement, which is where the profitability lies.

According to Steven Crist, "The issue is not which horse in the race is the most likely winner, but which horse or horses are offering odds that exceed their actual chances of victory. . . . Under this mindset everything but the odds fades from view" (Steven Crist, "Crist on Value," in Beyer et al., *Bet with the Best*, New York, Daily Racing Form Press, 2001). The key, then, is finding an attractive discrepancy between a horse's chances of winning and his price. You are looking for the best bet, not whether you like a horse.

So, what is it about our psychology that makes this so difficult? Why does it seem so hard to find original ideas that are nonconsensus? What must you do to become aware of your own psychology so that you can function independently of the way in which you are wired? How can you function in the realm of the unknown or in the realm of probabilities? What are the psychological traps that interfere with this process? What do you have to do to develop this "trader's edge" that I am talking about? It may all begin with *prospect theory* and our natural inclination toward risk aversion.

The prospect theory basically states that people do not assess probabilities based on theory. They tend to *overweight* low probabilities and *underweight* moderate and high probabilities. Our feelings about situations influence the way we weigh the probabilities. According to Daniel Kahneman and Mark Riepe: "The non-proportional weighting of probabilities makes people like both lottery tickets and insurance policies" (Daniel Kahneman and Mark W. Riepe, "Aspects of Investor Psychology: Beliefs,

Preferences and Biases Investment Advisors Should Know About," *Journal of Portfolio Management*, Vol. 24, No. 4, Summer 1998).

According to the *behavioral economics* approach to the markets, which led to a Nobel Prize for Daniel Kahneman, "given a choice between risky outcomes, human beings are twice as adverse to losses as to comparable gains" (Daniel Kahneman and Amos Tversky, "Prospect Theory: An Analysis of Decision Under Risk," *Econometrics*, No. 47, 1979, pp. 263–291).

Kahneman and co-author Amos Tversky found that most people demonstrate loss aversion in considering a gain or a loss. This psychological component accounts for the fact that people tend to hold onto losing trades as the trades go against them, taking more risk in the face of losses than might make sense in terms of risk-managing their portfolios. Likewise, they are inclined to take profits too soon on the positive side, again demonstrating less risk-taking propensity in a situation where they are likely to succeed.

In effect, the traders who have developed the trader's edge have learned to counter these hardwired psychological inclinations of risk aversion by learning to monitor their psychological responses to the market at the same time as they focus on the probability of the trade, irrespective of the emotional underpinning of most trades or in spite of their emotional wiring. In addition to this risk aversion, there are also other psychological factors operating within traders to inhibit them from reaching their ultimate level of success. Let me outline a few:

- **Framing:** How people perceive reference points regarding financial opportunities influences how people act. "Irrespective of the stock's perceived attractiveness, investors tend to sell the stocks above the purchase price and hold onto stocks below the purchase price," write Hersh Shefrin and Meir Statman ("The Disposition to Sell Winners Too Early and Ride Losers Too Long: Theory and Evidence," *Journal of Finance*, No. 40, 1985, pp. 777–790).
- **Overconfidence:** There is ample research indicating that people consistently overrate their abilities, knowledge, and skill, especially when it comes to areas outside their expertise.
- **Availability:** People tend to assess the frequency, probability, or likely cause of an event by their ability to recall other instances of its occurrence. Because we remember frequent events more easily, this pattern is likely to lead to bias in the kinds of data we use to support our choices.

- **Representativeness:** We often assess the likelihood of an event based on how similar the occurrence is to previous occurrences. This can lead to poor decision making with insufficient or incomplete information.

Racetrack handicappers are able to calibrate their predictions better by focusing on the same problems day after day, making explicit probabilistic predictions and getting precise and rapid feedback. But how can you overcome such behavioral biases and heuristic approaches to decision making? How can you overcome the tendency to poorly calibrate predictive statements?

First, it is important to understand the significance of time. It takes time for the process to produce results. If you do the right thing enough times, the results will take care of themselves. Process over immediate results is the key. Second, you have to look at your information.

There is no edge using public data or fundamental analysis. This kind of data and analysis tend to support consensus views. You can find this in the sell-side reports. It is the conventional thinking about a company, not original thinking based on a unique view of the possibility of the stock being a good bet. While sector supply/demand dynamics are key, there are numerous other factors that drive stocks that require "non-trend" analysis—for example, pension liability issues, options backdating, decisions on how to deploy excess cash, mergers and acquisitions (M&A), management changes, and accounting issues. These kinds of things need to be considered in addition to industry trends.

To get to the next level of expectational analysis, to really have a variant perception, an original view of what is possible that is not yet factored into the price of the stock, you need to be able to tap into psychology and sentiment and a variety of factors that make stocks move beyond the conventional numbers. You want to consider the context in which information is presented to evaluate the meaning of the data. Look for a broad range of inflection points over a potentially shorter time. Factor the variant view and time-weighted return into your methodology. Learn to recognize patterns in evaluating the value of data and make more accurate estimates.

This is an intuitive process and not strictly a left-brain or mathematical or fundamental process. The challenge is to be able to think originally and in terms of what is not immediately apparent. It is to trust your intuition and then develop the kind of research process that will support your hunch and not simply rely on conventional sources of information. You are looking for a path to getting paid, for determining what has to happen that will increase the probability of the success of your bet. This means focusing on what will increase your probability of success and what differentiates your approach to the investment as compared to others' approach.

Look for mispricings, disconnects, and other things that suggest that buying a company gives you a good shot at winning the bet in a reasonably well-defined time period, increasing your odds of winning. Recognize how much the market is based on irrational and emotional decisions and learn to be able to appreciate these tendencies by reading the chart action as well as by being able to assess the quality of information from suppliers, distributors, and others in the food chain.

Learn to understand human psychology, game theory, and behavioral finance phenomena. Assess the gap between the embedded price and what you know can happen and what you hope for. Consider what is in the stock and why the stock is inefficiently priced. What is the magnitude of expectations? The gap is proportional to the amount you expect to be paid. The larger the gap, the more you can make.

All of this may sound radically different to you. It is not the conventional approach that many traders have been led to follow. Can you change your stripes? Can you overcome the psychological hurdles and learn to trade this way, or do you have to be born with this kind of natural ability? Are some traders just naturally gifted with the trader's edge and others destined to struggle along hoping for a good day here and there? The answers to these questions are at the heart of this book.

Here I hope to define those things that seem to be inborn and those things that can be learned. I want to outline what steps you can take to move your game to the next level. I want you to understand where you have strengths and where you have weaknesses and how you can best utilize your natural tendencies. If you are evaluating new candidates for your fund, I want you as a hedge fund manager to understand how to look for and choose the best person for a job from the pool of highly talented individuals.

I am writing about the processes in which I am engaged, what I believe in, and how I help traders to produce extraordinary results. Using real-life examples from hedge fund managers and traders, everyday financial crises they face, interviews in which they discuss their own insecurities and exploit the inefficiencies in information, and personal trading profiles, I hope to enlighten you in regard to that "magic" formula we call *success*.

CHAPTER 1

Intellect, Instinct, and Guts

Understanding the Psychological Profile

At the age of 30, Charles Luckman was named president of the Pepsodent toothpaste company and later became president of Lever Brothers. Luckman knew from the age of nine that he wanted to be an architect but went into sales after graduating from the University of Illinois. Despite his great success in business, he eventually resigned from Lever Brothers to take up his architectural dream. From that point forward, he helped design such architectural wonders as the CBS Television City Center in Boston, the new Madison Square Garden in New York City and the NASA Manned Spacecraft Center in Houston. So, how did this businessman and architect who was once known as the "Boy Wonder of American Business" define *success*? "Success," Luckman said, "is that old ABC—ability, breaks, and courage."

Luckman's life was a remarkable demonstration of an amazingly simple yet complex formula for success, something that I have been searching for in my work with traders. For many years now, I have been trying to define the key ingredients of successful traders and portfolio managers (PMs) by exploring a range of personality strengths and weaknesses among them. To do this, I have asked such questions as:

- What are some of the different combinations of traits that contribute to individual success stories?
- How much "talent" is inborn, and what can be learned?

- How can hedge fund managers recognize talent and capitalize on it?
- Can talent be developed in individuals who are lacking natural ability?
- What are the developmental challenges that individuals must overcome if they are to develop into world-class performers?
- What attributes may look beneficial in the hiring process but then prove to be obstacles to success?
- Ultimately, what is the ideal configuration of intellect, instinct, and guts that, when blended, create the highest performers?

Along these lines, I was fortunate to talk to one of the premier hedge fund managers on Wall Street. During our interview, we discussed his views on the qualities that he believes make for the most successful analysts and portfolio managers in the business. This is what he had to say:

Kiev: What are the basic principles of trading success?

P: These are the principles that I put on the wall once I gave them that mythical line of credit. My number-one is to know names. I think there are a couple of ways to make mistakes. One is to fall in love with the concept or thesis before you know the name. We will live or die based on whether we know the names better than anybody else on the street.

K: Is that the variant perception?

P: It may not be variant; it may be reinforcing. I am on top of consensus on a couple of my longs, but I don't care because we are right. The market will have a lot of volatility. Some of that will be rational, and some of that will be stock prices leading you. Other than that, it will just be volatility. The reason the stock is down is because somebody else at a different organization is making a decision based on that person's viewpoint. It may have nothing to do with this stock. That's the dip that we are going to buy, and we are now going to fight this guy. He is selling; we are buying. How are we going to win that game? We are going to win that game if we know our names better.

K: How do you know it better?

P: You never really know you know it better, but we can tell whether we know our names holistically or whether we know our names intuitively. We can judge it relative to other names we know in our portfolio.

K: What do you mean *holistically* versus *intuitively*?

P: You have done all the work and you know the balance sheet, not only the numbers but also the business and how it works and the regulatory environment and the big changes in the business—not just a narrow subsegment.

Some of the analysts we had that didn't succeed here, that we had to let go, when we asked them to look at a name they would write the bull points and the bear points, all the obvious stuff. Then they would say, "I will buy a one percent position," or "I will short a one percent position," or "I would do nothing."

A pure listing of the bull points and the bear points is just a simulation. They are simulating that which Wall Street has told them or assimilating that which the company has told them. They are putting all the facts down on a page. They don't know that name. They have summarized the Cliff Notes from that name.

I would say that in eighty-five percent of investment organizations that's as far as they go. To know the name holistically is to do the other fifteen percent. So, when news comes out in which we have the best framework to interpret that news and make decisions as to whether this is nonsense or meaningful, whether this is underreaction or overreaction and how to move our portfolio, it all starts with, do we know our names? Do we know the industry?

Number two would be consistency. I need to remember this one as well. Sometimes we go into something saying, "We think for the next three years this company is structurally challenged. They are out of favor. Over the next three years, the company will not be able to perform. They cannot compound value. The stock is overvalued. Therefore, we think the stock is going to be down over forty percent over the next three years. It's just a question of when, and we want to short this stock." If we decided that's the case, then we need to be consistent. If they have a good quarter, who cares? There is a time over a thirty-six-month period when there is going to be a couple of good months. Who cares? There are going to be times when we aren't as long. There are going to be a couple of bad months. We cannot react to the twenty-five percent of data points that are good knowing that we have evaluated the landscape and that we know that seventy-five percent of the data points are going to be bad over time. That is a virtual certainty.

Number one, know your names. Number two, be consistent. Number three, ask yourself if your dollars have reflected your latest thinking.

K: Level of conviction?

P: I think a lot of times as the stock goes up, people like to have a bigger position because it's a happy name. If a stock has gone from thirty-two to thirty-eight dollars, on the one hand it's great, and you feel great about that name. But should you have twenty more dollars in that name today at thirty-eight? What really changed between point A and point B? Your story can get twenty percent better or in fact more than twenty percent better, but should it have more dollars allocated to that name at thirty-eight than you do at thirty-two? I think it's like comfort foods. We all know that if we eat comfort food, we get fat, and it's bad for us. Sometimes people just want to have it. It's the irrational, but they want to have it. Holding onto a winner without selling is like comfort food. People need to be willing to let go.

Number four would be "no opportunity equals zero cost." I think that some people get it in their minds that if they look at a stock and decide not to do anything and it goes up a hundred percent, then it cost them something. It cost them zero. They're not any poorer.

K: As opposed to beating themselves for missing it?

P: I think people are allocating capital in names because they think there is a possibility that this is a big stock, and they just don't want to miss it. So, they allocated a little more capital to the position. There is an instinct that we have to do a little more. They are afraid of the opportunity cost. So, those are my four cardinal rules.

K: How much are these rules rooted in fundamentals?

P: We are blessed and burdened with being rooted in the fundamentals. We are blessed with it because ultimately it helps us. We are burdened with it because it gives us conviction at times that may give us a sense of overconfidence. It's so tangible. We can all say tangibly the stock trading at six times earnings is cheap, but if other people are making decisions about less tangible things we will be blind to it.

K: What else would you teach a new analyst/PM?

P: When a guy comes in as an analyst, we teach him other things. We teach him how to communicate, how to stand up in the names, financial analysis, business analysis, how to do proprietary research and develop sources. This is what I would say to the guy: "You have graduated. Now you have your own pad. Here are the four cardinal rules. Before you make a capital allocation decision, I want you to go through this checklist."

K: You have guys that are smart analysts, that are the best of the best, and you think it's time to give them a portfolio. How would you assess whether a guy has what it takes to run a portfolio? How would you differentiate? Is there a decision-making gene, a risk-taking gene? A risk management gene, as opposed to just an analytic gene?

P: We critically refer to it as head, heart, and balls. You have got to have all three.

K: What does the PM have that the analyst doesn't have?

P: The analyst can only have a head and be a good analyst.

K: The PM has to have the heart and balls. Would you asses that from a guy's life experience? He played football or was a Navy Seal?

P: I think people who are leaders, entrepreneurs, are competitive, athletically or otherwise. I think that all those things can tell you something about that. Also, somebody can have a perfect resume, you know, undergraduate at Yale, went to McKinsey, did a Harvard MBA, went to Goldman Sachs. I look at it and say, "The guy has never taken a risk in his life. This guy wants to be the middle-of-the-road guy. He is proficient. He would be a great manager. He may even be a great analyst, but it's totally unproven as to whether he is a risk taker and a risk manager."

K: Could he be taught that, or is it genetics or DNA? Would you take that Goldman Sachs guy?

P: I am not sure if you start learning it at thirty-four years old—it may be starting too late. You can teach an adult to ice skate, but it's a lot easier to teach a five-year-old. He is going to be a better, more natural skater over time.

I don't think that I was born with a risk gene. I think I learned risk management because I started gambling on horses and making probability bets when I was a kid. I think I was competitive because I was playing hockey, and that just became my nature. I think that those were all learned responses. I wasn't born with those. They were learned from the time I was young.

Can you teach somebody who has come through one path for forty years to take a different turn? I don't know. I don't think so. I can tell on that organization chart that we have some guys who are phenomenally good. For example, one analyst is the proverbial example I gave you. He is a Yale undergraduate. He went to Merrill Lynch investment banking, and then he came here. He succeeded in everything he did. He had a four-point-oh GPA. You give him a complex problem, he goes away. He comes back, and he knows everything. I don't want to glass-ceiling him, but I have no idea if he will ever be a good trader or a good risk manger. I have an enormous amount of confidence that he is going to be a terrific analyst. So, I view him as someday a director of research but not a portfolio manager.

K: Could you pick someone who you would say could become a portfolio manager?

P: Yeah, Brandon.

K: What does he have that is different from the Yale grad?

P: They both have an emotional balance. They are true to themselves, and they are centered. They are consistent. They are self-confident. They have a framework. They are incredibly detail-oriented. You know a lot of people look at the pieces of the puzzle and see what's there. You also need to see what's *not* there and what's missing. I think they have great vision and have great ears. I think they are self-competent. It's hard to figure out what the differential skills are. It may just simply be a practicality about them. I think that a great analyst is prone to be over-theoretical. Whereas I think a great portfolio manager is immensely practical. It's not about whether it's fair or unfair that the stock goes up or down based on the fundamentally technical or other reasons. They look at it practically.

My job is to make investment decisions that are going to be profitable. I think that an analyst is prone to believe in hindsight that the market made a mistake and he didn't. Whereas I think a portfolio manager is inclined to look at the situation and say, "What can I draw upon to improve?" In terms of pattern recognition, you need to go back and figure out what the pattern was that you should have seen.

K: Which the analyst may be reluctant to do.

P: The analyst may be more narrow-minded in his thinking and just become exasperated. He may think, "I have hit every earnings estimate that I have ever had. Why am I not making money?"

K: So, what if you have a guy with an incredible resume? What does he need beyond the resume that can be picked up in an interview and review of his history?

P: He can be an idealist. He has to be comfortable and define his job, not from an intellectual perspective, but from a practical perspective. He would need to understand that everything is seated at the table.

What are the basic principles of success? Are there specific genes that make success easier for some than for others? Are some people cut out for some positions for which others are not? Can principles of success, like those outlined earlier, be learned or forced? These were the questions that were discussed. The answers are worth considering when evaluating anyone for employment in a hedge fund as an analyst or portfolio manager. But the answers aren't cut and dry.

The measure of someone's potential success can perhaps never be completely known, but a lot can be discovered through a careful review of psychological tests, personal history, and intense interviews in which the individual's life experiences, past professional experiences, and ways of dealing with risk, stress, life events, success, and failure can be evaluated in order to determine a person's characteristic ways of functioning in the world.

A *psychological profile* can be created in various ways, using standardized psychological tests, interviews, reference checks, and the like. Whatever tests you use, it is important that you consider certain dimensions of behavior I believe are critical to a trader's edge. These include how well a trader:

- Makes decisions
- Generates ideas
- Handles adversity
- Manages himself and others
- Sets and works toward goals
- Conceptualizes and engages in abstract reasoning
- Personally engages in action in his approach to work
- Solves problems and makes decisions
- Generates creative ideas about the instruments and companies being traded
- Takes risk in an appropriate way
- Leads and empowers others in pursuit of stretch goals and targets

You also want to evaluate how an individual handles research projects you give him to assess the quality of his work, his diligence, his ability to think creatively, and his sense of urgency and thoroughness. How receptive is he to criticism? How original is his thought process? Take your time here and do not rush to judgment. This real-time evaluation will give you more color on how he is likely to adapt to your team than what you might glean from the interview process. Such a comprehensive review can be used to assess an individual and make probabilistic predictions as to how he is likely to behave in the future in the context of the risk-taking required for working in a hedge fund or financial institution.

By exploring these themes, I have been able to increase my ability to determine whether a candidate has the requisite personality that will succeed in this business or in a particular facet of this business. These characteristics also provide a template for reviewing the performance of existing portfolio managers, as well as hedge fund managers who are trying to take their performance to the next level.

A HISTORY OF SUCCESS

The fundamentals of education and work experience are just a beginning. In order to develop a true psychological profile and determine whether a candidate has the trader's edge, you must consider his history of success. What is a history of success? As cliché as it may sound, you will know a history of success when you hear it. Success manifests itself in a number of ways. For example, it could be the story of a young Russian immigrant with one year of high school who arrived in the states and one year later received a full scholarship to a pre–Ivy League prep school, followed by a magna cum laude degree from an Ivy League college, making his way to M&A at a major investment bank and eventually trading convertible bonds at a $1 billion hedge fund. But success can also be found in the candidate who was a Rhodes scholarship winner and played on his country's Davis team representing his country in international competition. Basically, a history of success connotes drive, goal-directedness, conscientiousness, and discipline.

Of course, you can also gain a lot of information from reference checks. I want to know how good a candidate is relative to all the people with whom the reference has worked. I am looking for superlative assessments that sound like the following report on Richard, given by a senior portfolio manager who had worked with him at his previous position:

Richard was a "tremendous hire" and a "perfect candidate" and he could not recommend him more strongly. He described Richard as "smart, talented, thoughtful, methodical" and, importantly, a good guy and someone with whom he enjoyed working. He claimed that Richard is among the top 2% of people he has ever trained given how quickly he got up to speed and the quality of the questions and thoughtfulness of his remarks. He believes Richard's prospects and future are unlimited. "Richard knows a lot, is humble about what he doesn't know, understands risks, understands the markets, deals well with disappointment and has a ton of common sense. He will be an immediately impactful portfolio manager."

I recommend talking to several people about a candidate and trying to size him up relative to his peers as well as sizing up the person giving the reference, how well he understands what you are looking for, and how broad his base is in making positive statements about a candidate. The more focused your questions, based on any kind of apparent contradictions or problems that may have surfaced in the course of your enquiry, the more valuable the reference call can be in sizing up an individual's will power and desire for success, which are intangible but critical ingredients of success in a high-tension, high-risk financial trading environment.

THE ABILITY TO TAKE RISK

In the hedge fund universe, one's ability to take risk is essential. In effect, you must be able to assess the individual's capacity to function in terms of outsized performance targets, his ability to listen, and his ability to incorporate and process critical feedback about his performance by reviewing risk statistics with the risk manager so as to find ways of changing his trading and portfolio management behavior in order to improve his overall performance. The individual's past history can provide a clue as to how he is going to handle decision making in situations where he has insufficient information, how well he will be able to build a team, and how he is going to manage toward greater performance. If an individual is too cautious or too thorough, or in a psychological sense too perfectionistic, he is likely to have difficulty in adapting to a goal-oriented, high-performance approach to portfolio management and as such might not be a good candidate. In addition, it is important to screen out traders who are too impulsive, impatient, and perhaps irrational risk-takers and lack sufficient cautiousness and thoroughness to keep from blowing up.

By looking at a trader's profitability, or P&L, his percentage of winning trades, his slugging ratio or W/L ratio, as well as his Sharpe ratio and other risk statistics from his previous job, it is possible to identify certain behavioral patterns that are reflective of his overall past performance (i.e., whether he doesn't take enough risk, takes too much, is not balanced, doesn't cull his losers, doesn't get bigger in his winners—a lot of which is secondary to underlying psychological patterns). Given this information, you can make certain assumptions about his future performance.

Of course, the successful trader in essence is a goal-oriented risk-taker with good abstract reasoning and not too much cautiousness or thoroughness that might interfere with his ability to trade stocks in his portfolio, unless he is a long-term value investor. In that case, his cautiousness and thoroughness may support the kind of portfolio strategy he has developed to do very thorough work, to buy stocks when they are cheap, and to hold them for long periods of time as they mature in value.

CREATIVITY AND ORIGINALITY

Most of us are driven more by consensus than by thinking outside the box. In order to make money in the markets, a trader needs to know something that others don't know yet. So, when you are considering a candidate's potential, you must think about his thought processes.

- Does he have the ability to think abstractly and creatively and to make predictions based on imperfect and incomplete information?
- Can he function in the realm of the variant perception, where he sees nonconsensus, nonlinear, and creative investment opportunities?
- Does he have a high tolerance for ambiguity and uncertainty and a willingness to dig in deeply to understand more about a company and its product cycles, or margin expansions, or management changes or other drivers of value, than anyone else in the world?
- Is he comfortable with nonconsensus viewpoints?
- Does he take pride in his ability to function quite independently of the herd?

The ability to do this is clearly helped by the quality of work done to support investment efforts. When a trader has a high degree of abstract reasoning ability and the ability to think creatively, he is more likely to generate original investment ideas at a sufficient velocity to keep pace with allocated capital and stretch targets.

The successful trader should also be able to troubleshoot and solve problems in his area of expertise. Ideally, he should be decisive, especially when there is limited information to make an investment decision or to take calculated risks. He should be able to assess complex situations, identify the drivers influencing transformative events in companies or other variables that may influence the stock price of companies he is buying, and be able to determine the appropriate answers when there are a range of possible solutions to a given problem. He should be flexible and adaptable based on the arrival of new information and not become fixed in a position because of previous analyses. This should give him a variety of ways to handle situations.

To the extent that the trader has good abstract reasoning ability and is conceptually oriented, he should be able to adapt to a variety of situations and come up with original solutions. Most of all, he needs to be able to function with limited information and to deal with the unforeseen events in the future without guarantees or certainty. He should be comfortable with dealing with improbable events or the tails of events rather than having to rely on the consensus or conventional ways of approaching problems. Having a variant perception and doing the work to support it is a key to success.

SELF-AWARENESS, SELF-CONTROL, AND RESILIENCE

Emotional obstacles such as anxiety and fear are compounded in the daily world of trading because of the uncertainty of the markets. A successful trader therefore needs to be able to notice and separate his emotional responses from the decisions that he is making. He should be able to reach a centered state where he is able to see the movement of the market without becoming reactive to it.

Many people trick themselves into believing false notions about themselves and their abilities. Because of a lack of information or an inability to correctly assess the information they have, they either overvalue their abilities—thinking they are far better at certain tasks than they really are—or undervalue their potential—falling prey to insecurities and poor self-esteem. This is demonstrated very dramatically when I sit down with the risk manager to review a trader's risk statistics and discover how much the trader is in denial about his actual trading performance.

To combat this kind of denial, use trading statistics to provide a snapshot of the underlying behavioral dynamics of the trader's trading patterns, the capacity of the trader to handle and recover from failure, and the ability to turn breakdowns into breakthroughs. The tolerance for failure and the capacity to recover from failure and adversity are major characteristics of the successful trader since most PMs are right only 60 percent of the time and as such must be able to continue to function even though they may be wrong 40 percent of the time. This provides value in exploring thoroughly the individual's past experience with success, and evidence in his life of stretching, going for the gold, and seeking to win over adversity.

A successful trader also has the ability to function on his own, to find and develop ideas, to find sources of support within a firm or in the sellside community, and to stay disciplined and on target. He generally prefers to function with some degree of independence and autonomy and as such functions best in environments that give him some latitude in making investment decisions. At the same time, he is aware of the need for some structure and is not so independent that he cannot function within the boundaries of good risk management principles or whatever other guidelines are provided and expected by the firm. The best PM will have a well-developed balance between his sense of urgency to get things done and achieve his goals and the need to do this in a balanced way so that he does not make mistakes because of haste or over-enthusiasm. This kind of PM is a responsible and conscientious individual who is thorough and accurate in the way he approaches his tasks, although at times he may require some support from others to help set priorities.

Teaching Traders Self-Assessment and Self-Control

Not every trader instinctively knows how to monitor his emotions. In fact, you may find this ability to be one of the hardest to discover among potential candidates. Fortunately, it is one that can be taught.

First, encourage traders to keep a log of their trades. They should record exactly what took place in a given trade and how they responded to it. For example, say they bought a stock at 20. They planned to do a little more work to take a larger position, but it started to move against them. By logging their emotions as well as the physical manifestations of the trade, they can review exactly what they were experiencing. They can consider how they were feeling and how those feelings affected their reactions. Did they get out at the appropriate time? Did they hang on in false hope? Was their decision an emotional one, or was it based on data?

By keeping track of this during trading and later reviewing the trades, they will become more aware of how emotional responses influence their trading. By developing a consciousness about these responses, they will be more likely to observe the repetitiveness of their actions and not act impulsively.

TEAMWORK AND LEADERSHIP

To the extent that he is building a portfolio and increasing the amount of capital in his portfolio, the successful trader will also be someone who shows evidence of leadership ability, especially when it comes time to expand his team of analysts to assist him in finding more ideas and doing more work on those in his portfolio. To be a good team leader he ideally will have the right amount of empathy required to understand the needs of those he is managing and a capacity for gregariousness and sociability that will enable him to interact successfully with others and to empower them to become all they are capable of becoming. To some extent, this capacity also relates to the PM's ability to be coached himself and to work on improving his own game by learning from others, by being flexible and accommodative to the needs and vision of the organization.

The best PMs have a capacity for leadership and teamwork that is evidenced by their ability to suppress their egos and empower others. They are less egocentric and more empathetic and empowering of others.

While a successful PM may be making investment decisions on his own within the risk management parameters of his firm, he may be called on to function with others in a collaborative way, sharing ideas and best practices, empowering others, and accepting coaching as it relates to his own performance. The introspective, highly intellectual but withdrawn or reticent individual may be a brilliant contributor but may not function as well in certain environments that encourage interaction with others. It is important that the PM have the ability to establish rapport with others and build relationships on the job. He ought to be receptive to feedback from those around him and willing to listen and consider different viewpoints. Does he want to be liked and respected? Does he appreciate thanks for his efforts, or does he function so independently that it is hard to envision him as contributing to a team effort?

How does he view the intentions of others? Is he a bit skeptical about their intentions? Does he question their motives? Does it take a long time for him to trust other people? How willing is he to give people the benefit of the doubt? These are critical variables that need to be considered and that can be garnered from the individual's past history and reference checks.

To the extent that the successful trader is someone who ultimately may need to size his portfolio to handle more capital and to build a team of analysts to increase the velocity of ideas, it is desirable that he has some leadership potential as well. To what extent does this PM have the self-assurance, persuasive drive, and assertiveness to overcome resistance and gain support for his vision? How resilient is he in handling resistance, rejection, or negative feedback so that he can stay focused on his goals without going into default negativity or excessive aggressiveness? How well can he handle conflict, and to what extent does he need to dominate the direction of events? Does change create problems for him? How good is he at issuing directives and motivating people to act in terms of his objectives and plans? How much empathy does he have? How able is he to understand where people are coming from and how best to incorporate their views into his directives and efforts to empower them?

Such behaviors require an ability to stand outside oneself and one's concerns about image in order to function in terms of larger objectives. Whereas an introvert may be able to look at companies and manage a portfolio, he might lack the people skills necessary to develop levels of empathy and sociability to be able to engage others and to want to lead them. Such a person may have trouble being able to scale and manage a team of analysts.

Finally, how do all these characteristics combine to make for effective leadership, balancing urgency for results with the need to involve others in a proactive and supportive way? To what extent does the candidate apply his own high standards not only to himself but to others, and is this productive or counterproductive? How much effort must he make to reconcile or balance his own needs with the needs of his team? Can he motivate others without being too critical or overpowering? The strong leader needs to be able to temper his own objectives with the need to provide enough freedom for his colleagues to be able to develop their own abilities.

PUTTING IT ALL TOGETHER

Obviously the assessment of the ingredients of a successful portfolio manager takes into consideration a variety of characteristics. The more you consider this range of qualities in evaluating potential candidates for your firm and in assessing the ongoing performance of those already working for you, the more conversant you will become with these critical psychological dimensions of evaluating human beings both in advance and during the time they are working with you in your firm. The more practice you have, the better you will get at sizing up how these differing characteristics actually manifest themselves in individuals, and how some blend and others neutralize the impact of certain characteristics. Over time, you will develop greater sensitivity about the kinds of things that make for stellar performance, which ones are stubbornly retained, which ones can be molded by training, and which ones work best in your particular organization. This is not meant to be the Holy Grail, but it does provide a larger conceptual framework for evaluating people so that eventually you are able to hire the right kind of people who will thrive in your organization.

CASE STUDY ON FINDING THE RIGHT CANDIDATE

Let's put all of this into action and consider candidates for an imaginary position. For example, imagine you are trying to find the ideal candidate for a portfolio manager's position.

Job Requirements

This job requires the candidate to provide in-depth fundamental analysis within his industry sector. He will develop financial models to predict company performance, assess event drivers within the sector, stay current with a range of sector companies to anticipate market moves, and be able to act appropriately in building a portfolio, sizing positions commensurate with his level of conviction and consistent with stretch targets that will be developed in conversation with the risk management team. He will work in a thorough manner, generate conclusions, and present findings with conviction. Then he must be able to populate a balanced portfolio in line with his varying levels of conviction. He should also use a proactive, instinctive approach to identify investment opportunities.

In addition, he will develop a detailed research and investment analysis process using proprietary financial models, valuation, and edge/outcome analysis as part of a streamlined approach to investment. He should be able to manage a team of research professionals and help direct the team into investment areas on which to focus. His research process should be a rigorous bottom's-up research and analysis of industries and companies to provide buy/sell/hold recommendations. He should also be able to create a portfolio and follow appropriate risk management techniques within the firm's investment framework. Having looked at a large number of portfolio managers, some successful and some not so successful, I would say that based on the above listed considerations, the best candidate would have:

- An outstanding academic pedigree and professional history of success
- Outstanding abstract reasoning ability and the ability to think creatively and originally
- A natural capacity for risk-taking
- A self-starter personality with drive, ego strength, and resilience
- Interpersonal skills, which make for leadership and team play
- A coachable personality

Additionally, I would look for an individual with some in-depth knowledge of the drivers of businesses, a capacity to do basic fundamental analytical work, and a passion and drive to learn about the long/short public markets. To the extent that an individual from the private equity world might have no experience trading in the public equity space, I would be interested in whether the individual has had any experience trading a personal account, although this is a secondary consideration when the rest of the pedigree and history is outstanding.

Potential Candidates

We have three potential candidates: Dennis, Peter, and Toby. Let's get to know each one and determine which is the best fit for this position.

Dennis Dennis is a smart guy. He is a very focused and determined individual who requires little guidance and attention to accomplish the task at hand. He is very deliberate and conscientious but will only assume risk that is calculated. Once he has done the necessary work and analysis, he will confidently state his opinion and will be objective in his recommendations. He sets high standards for himself and likes to chart his own course and do his own thing.

As such, Dennis is not motivated by engaging with others, supporting others, or operating as a member of a team. He is distrustful of other traders' work and contributions and prefers to operate independently and contribute autonomously to an effort. He is neither sociable nor particularly gregarious and does not value developing and training others.

Peter Based on our assessment of Peter on a number of occasions, our own interview with him, repeated phone conversations, a review of his work experience, a personality profile, and due diligence with people who worked for him and with him, and for whom he worked, it has been our impression that he is an engaging, ambitious, self-aware, self-starter who is a measured and thorough risk-taker with an extremely high level of abstract reasoning ability (both in terms of doing math in his head and solving abstract problems). He is very curious, analytical, ambitious, and competitive. He has an in-depth knowledge of the space in which he worked for ten years and high leadership potential. He has both short and long-term objectives, including the ability to integrate very complex concepts and a variety of financial instruments, such that once he learns the long/short public equity markets he will be able to leverage his private equity experience and add considerable value to his own portfolio management activities as well as those of the firm. Despite his lack of experience in the public markets, Peter has an enormous amount of self-awareness and the humility to understand the work it will take to get up to speed so that he is functioning as brilliantly in long/short public equity portfolio management as he has functioned in the private equity space from which he came.

While there would clearly be a learning curve for Peter in terms of understanding how to trade publically traded stocks, his previous success indicates that he will learn quickly. He is eager to learn, open to different interpretations, and enjoys seeking out the information and knowledge necessary to build the required skill set.

His primary reference, Dale, could not speak to his risk tolerance per se but equated *risk tolerance* with Peter's tendency to think outside the box and propose a variant view on companies. Dale, who worked very closely with Peter at his previous firm, indicated that Peter did not need to follow the pack in terms of his recommendations and instead looked at every investment decision with a fresh lens and his own process. He also mentioned that Peter has grown into a deeper maturity regarding his investment approach and in his reactions to and tolerance for mistakes. Dale said that early on in Peter's career, Peter had an aversion to discussing or revisiting names that had failed him, that he would essentially "bury his head and pretend it [the loss] wasn't happening." However, Peter has since developed an ability to learn from his mistakes and "over time has learned to examine these situations very closely, conduct a forensic-type analysis of the mistakes to better understand what went wrong, where his thinking was off, where in the life cycle of the idea he miscalculated, and determine areas where he could improve and learn. This has made him a wiser, more confident, more flexible and adaptive investor."

Toby   Toby is a very smart analyst and assistant portfolio manager in a large hedge fund. He worked there for ten years and developed a lot of knowledge in international technology stocks. In fact, he generated buy-and-sell ideas for many overseas companies in which his fund currently has a couple of billion-dollar investments. For the past several years, Toby has been responsible for the portfolio management of the technology portion of an overseas fund that has produced annualized returns of more than 35 percent. During this time, fund assets have grown from $3 billion to $11 billion. He has experience in developing elaborate company models and in planning for and meeting with CEOs of companies.

He is an extremely bright magna cum laude graduate of Dartmouth, a very pleasant fellow, albeit a bit nervous and socially awkward. He has limited experience in managing others but has taught classes at Dartmouth and managed a few people while at a consulting firm.

After meeting with him, we found that, although very bright and knowledgeable, Toby had a long-term time horizon and might take some time learning to short and to assess companies for shorter-term catalysts and the path to getting paid. Although Toby knew his sector well, he tended to focus more on the big picture (one to two years out) than he would need to in a shorter time horizon, long/short, public equity–oriented hedge fund. Whereas he knew what he owned extremely well in terms of what they do and what the drivers of the stocks are, it would be a big adjustment for Toby to short stocks, something he had never really done in the mutual fund world. Previous experience indicates that it sometimes takes as much as two to three years for people to make this adjustment. Toby might also find it to be a big adjustment in managing his longs because he was so inclined to take such a long view. As it stands, Toby's ideas would be diffi-cult for the firm to leverage unless he changed his style.

Digging in more deeply, I explored Toby's capacity to be trained, his motivation to succeed, and his willingness to be part of a team to determine whether he was a viable candidate. What I found was interesting and chal-lenging. Toby's profile shows that he is smart, a risk-taker, open to others' opinions, and flexible in his approach to things. He is extremely confident in himself. Because of this, it may appear as though he is not open and not listening but in fact he will attend to other people, particularly if he believes that they will be instructive in making him successful. He is focused, dis-ciplined, and structured and has a balanced profile, displaying aggressive risk-taking as well as judgment and some cautiousness. However, he does not seem driven or motivated by reaching out to others, building relation-ships, and working for the benefit of others. From a coaching standpoint, Toby is trainable provided there is someone very strong-willed to coach and develop him. He would need someone who is strong enough to push back and refute his views as he is accustomed to being right (or at least to believing that he is right).

The Bottom Line

Of these three, Peter is by far the best candidate. The concerns regard-ing Dennis center on his interpersonal and leadership skills. While his cur-rent role as an analyst does not require strong leadership (necessarily), Dennis's lack of team orientation, partnership skills, and general interest in motivating and coaching others could limit his potential if he were to be considered for a portfolio manager role or to manage a team of analysts.

Toby is also a very smart guy, but at this point is a square peg for a round hole. In order for him to work out, he would have to change his investment style. Given that there is a large component of the role that is new to him (shorting), a question remains as to whether he will be too confident and too self-involved to seek out others for his own learning.

Hopefully, this example helps you to understand how to assimilate a variety of information on a number of candidates. Remember, traders are in a constant search for information that will provide a clue as to what will happen next, but even more important than the facts that they find are the ways in which those facts are digested. How are the details being perceived? How are investors reacting to the information? By consider-ing these types of profiles, you can find evidence as to how each person will, generally speaking, react to various circumstances. By making considerations such as those discussed here, you can more readily determine a candidate's ability to succeed.

THE PERFECT CANDIDATE?

Is there really an ideal candidate, one who has all the "perfect" ingredients I have outlined in this chapter and throughout this book? Perhaps; but it should also be noted that some very successful people have only a few of these traits. The goal is to look for people who have as many of these characteristics as can be found. I am also advocating that other people develop some of their strengths along these lines. But, it is still important to recognize that some people have the X factor, and though they might not meet my idealized criteria, they might nevertheless be quite successful at trading. As with most of my books, this information is presented as a set of useful concepts from which to judge your own experience and what you need to do to improve your selection of PMs for your firm or improve your game if you are the PM yourself.

I think it is also important to understand that each person has his or her own style of trading and preparation. Clearly, when you look at people who have been successful over the years, you find a variety of profiles. Indeed, the more profiles you review, the more you realize the complexity of personalities and the value of digging deeper, exploring the potential fit of people you hire into your organization.

I recognize that there is not one single personality profile that is correlated with successful investing. Some people are strong in abstract reasoning and mathematics. Others have a gift for intuitively reading the movements of markets. Still others are skilled at managing teams of analysts because of their extroverted personality and their sensitivity to the levers that motivate people. The reason we assess personality is to find various combinations of talents that in our experience seem to increase the chances of success. While we are continually paying attention to the basic potential that each trader seems to have, at the end of the day, perseverance, experience, drive, and a variety of factors sometimes serve to compensate for apparent weaknesses in personality and natural talent. Passion, heart, and commitment are all very difficult variables to measure, but they are perhaps the most critical attributes for success.

CHAPTER IN REVIEW

1. While no one single personality profile is correlated with successful investing, we can find various combinations of talents that seem to increase the chances of success by carefully:

   - Reviewing a person's psychological tests, personal history, life experiences, past professional experiences, and ways of dealing with risk, stress, life events, success, and failure

   - Conducting intense interviews and carefully considering reference checks

   - Evaluating how an individual handles research projects to assess the quality of his work, his diligence, his ability to think creatively, and his sense of urgency and thoroughness

   - Considering his capacity to function in terms of outsized performance targets, his ability to listen, and his ability to incorporate and process critical feedback about his performance by reviewing risk statistics

   - Examining his thought processes, his ability to troubleshoot, solve problems, assess complex situations, and identify the drivers influencing transformative events in companies

2. A few of the most important attributes of a successful trader are:

   - The ability to notice and separate emotional responses from the decision-making process

   - The ability to function with some degree of independence and autonomy while still following good risk management principles

   - The ability to stand outside oneself and one's concerns about images in order to function in terms of larger objectives

   - The ability to suppress ego and empower others to share ideas and best practices and accept coaching

3. Perseverance, experience, drive, and a variety of factors sometimes serve to compensate for apparent weaknesses in personality and natural talent.

CHAPTER 2

Planning for Action

The Importance of Goal-Directedness

Until one is committed there is hesitancy, the chance to draw back, always ineffectiveness. Concerning all acts of initiative (and creation), there is one elementary truth, the ignorance of which kills countless ideas and splendid plans: that the moment one definitely commits oneself, then Providence moves too. All sorts of things occur to help one that would never otherwise have occurred. A whole stream of events issues from the decision, raising in one's favour all manner of unforeseen incidents and meetings and material assistance, which no man could have dreamt would come his way. Whatever you can do, or dream you can, begin it. Boldness has genius, power and magic in it.

—W. H. Murray, Scottish Himalayan
Expedition leader

I find a lot of inspiration in this quote from the Scottish Himalayan Expedition's leader, W. H. Murray, about the power of taking action toward specific objectives. This is the way humans first learn to do most things in life, by deliberately planning every move. When a toddler learns to walk, each step is tentative. He must think about every move. When a teenager learns to drive, each decision is conscious—turn on the ignition,

29

put the car in gear, press the gas slowly. . . . To learn sports and then to play at maximum levels, athletes consciously and deliberately perform each action. Eventually, however, toddlers, teenagers, and athletes, as well as traders, begin to perform seemingly difficult tasks skillfully with hardly any thought at all. With enough practice, even the most difficult tasks will eventually become second nature, almost effortless.

When a trader reaches that level of unconcerned action, where he has learned what to do and has sustained a certain level of performance, then it is time to move forward. To reach a greater level of performance requires greater consciousness, a renewed focus, and a detailed plan. Success won't come without effort.

MAKING A PLAN

Scientific research illustrates how action plans help people achieve their goals. Dr. Peter Gollwitzer, Professor of Psychology at New York University, has conducted several studies that demonstrate the benefits of making specific plans that outline when, where, and how to perform an action (*The Psychology of Action: Linking Cognition and Motivation to Behavior*, edited by Peter M. Gollwitzer and John A. Bargh, New York: Guilford Press, 1998). For example, a trader will find it useful to determine beforehand that when Market Condition X happens and Pattern Y appears, then he should enter at a prescribed moment, set a protective stop, and monitor the trade until Z occurs. Knowing when, where, and how helps him perform more gracefully. Specific plans help traders respond quickly and automatically when it is necessary. Without a plan, traders can expect less in the way of results and more hassles.

Take, for example, Benjamin, an execution trader who was running a small pad of his own. Whereas Benjamin obviously wanted to make money and even discussed his desire to make money, he went into a drawdown early in the year and took months to recover. His mistake was to pursue the strategy of buy and hold that had been successful the previous year and not shift to more active trading and taking of profits.

While Benjamin demonstrated an ability to size high-conviction ideas, he failed to set a goal and define a strategy consistent with changing market conditions that would help him produce a solid P&L. When pressed, he acknowledged that over the next three years he would like to become a portfolio manager and manage more money. He realizes that to meet this goal, he needs to establish some specific steps. He must:

- Get out of his comfort zone.
- Work harder (meet with six analysts per week rather than just one or two).
- Overcome his sense of inadequacy about "not being an analyst."
- Recognize that he has something to offer as a guy who is in touch with the trading flow, and learn to leverage the firm's platform.
- Be more willing to seek the support of others.

These are very specific steps that he can take in pursuit of his goal. In addition, he is going to start a dialogue with appropriate individuals in order to get a better feel for what is going on in his space, start writing up his daily notes on market flow and information, and start sending more e-mails with the idea of increasing the number of high-conviction ideas (looking for five stocks in which he could take 12 percent positions as opposed to one where he was taking a 20 percent position), all in an effort to increase his P&L and eventually grow his capital.

Like Benjamin, if you have a clearly defined plan, you will be more ready to respond efficiently in circumstances relating to the achievement of your goal. In addition, when you have a plan, you can more easily ignore interruptions and distractions and realize where your resources are lacking.

The human mind has limitations. We can attend to only a limited amount of information at a time. A detailed trading plan, which includes a unique variant perception and the path to getting paid, within the framework of a solid risk management methodology that is consistent with producing outperformance (what I consider the trader's edge), allows traders to focus limited psychological energy more efficiently. Basically, if you want to trade like a winner, make a detailed trading plan and follow it.

CASE STUDY ON SETTING A GOAL

How do you go about setting a goal? Review what you have done in the past. See what is repeatable. Consider the resources available to you. Understand the firm's standards and set a goal that is a stretch for you but not unrealistic. Then divide the annual goal into monthly or weekly targets. For example, if you have a $1-million-per-month goal on $50 million of capital, you should ask yourself what you would need to accomplish *weekly* in order to meet that goal. You need to define what specific steps will be needed to reach your goal. This can be done by addressing three areas: quality of work, risk management, and discipline. More specifically, consider to what extent your ideas reflect a variant perception. Are you appropriately sizing your high-conviction ideas? How well-developed are your research and portfolio management processes?

To understand this process better, let's consider the case of Stan, who has been struggling for several years to become a portfolio manager. He has had trouble learning how to manage risk and recently gave up $1.7 million in profit in several positions. In an effort to modify his approach, he has worked up a new methodology, planning to attend selected meetings, targeting $1 million/month on $50 million of capital, and focusing on risk management issues. He believes that he can turn it around and has outlined the following steps to help him do so:

1. **Regarding quality of work:** Stan plans to travel as much a possible to meet with companies and go to trade shows to generate ideas. He is going to focus on names that are under-followed or where he can develop an edge. He is going to generate one high-conviction long and one high-conviction short each week and make sure to get feedback regarding those ideas.

2. **Regarding risk management:** He is going to cut losses faster. If a position is down 10 percent, he is going to cut it in half. If it is down 20 percent, he is going to get out. Stan is going to review and highlight where each position is at the end of every day and focus on sizing. He plans on making sure each position is a max of one day volume unless it is a catalyst-driven idea with a specific date in mind. In those cases, he will write up and communicate his reason for sizing.

3. **Regarding discipline:** Stan plans to follow the above processes and also develop a weekly write-up of management discussions and quarterly previews.

Stan went on to chart each month's capital, the target goal, the number of trading days, the number of positions he needed to put on, and the amount of profit per day and per position that he would need to make to reach his goal. He also made a list of upcoming events that would help him build conviction. I encouraged him to take the process a step further and to outline his top five positions and what he expected from them in the coming year. He researched what his top five ideas were, their current targets, the increase, the profit increase, and the timing.

Stan considered all of these critical components, but somehow he wasn't able to put it together. After following this plan for six months, he had not really performed as well as he might have, and it was decided that he added more value as an analyst than as a portfolio manager; perhaps he had taken on this added responsibility of running a portfolio prematurely. Today he is doing quite nicely as an analyst and spending all of his time digging deeply.

Stan's experience is interesting and contrasts quite nicely with the more elaborate model developed by Jeremy, who spent several more years learning to be a more developed analyst and running a carve-out under an experienced PM before he began to run his own book. You can see from his process what a more developed approach looks like.

Jeremy has taken the goal-setting process to another level. What follows is an outline of Jeremy's extensive efforts to establish a variant view in the companies he is investing in and to bolster that edge by doing the necessary original work to support that view.

1. Understand your sector. Find something that is changing, a transformative event, and figure out what it will be worth when the value of the stock is fully realized. Consider, for example, whether there is a contemplated sale of a division followed by a buyback of stock with the money gained from the sale, or whether there is an acquisition or some new event that will transform the company and unlock value, and figure out the timing and when your expectations will be realized. Keep looking for setups such as a buyback, earnings beats, and other transformative events.

2. Do the work that will increase your conviction that your expectations will be realized. If there are real corporate changes, and they are selling a division and buying back stock, the math is simple and cookie-cutter.

3. If people underestimate the value of the company going forward, look at what happened in the past when the company beat numbers. Did people care? Did it move the stock price? Rely more on historical events when you don't have a simple math formula.

4. Don't worry about day-to-day price fluctuations if your thesis is correct. Don't worry about exogenous events if your thesis is correct.

5. Essentially define the variant view and set up some benchmarks to see whether your thesis is playing out. It is not so important as to whether

stock is cheap (e.g., 10× earnings or 11× earnings). It is more important to consider whether it is earning $10 and you think it will earn $20. Can you do the work to increase your probability of success? In essence, a change in numbers is more useful to determine than simple valuations.

6. All of this can be supported by technical analysis, but remember that technical analysis often creates a self-fulfilling prophecy. Nevertheless, there is value in chart support, understanding the price of oils, and synergies from what others are saying. All of this acts as redundancies to support your thesis and increase the number of reasons why you will be paid.

7. It is important to get sized with good ideas and let the idea mature even if you have got only one or two datapoints. You have to think bigger than your own limited set of datapoints. It is important to learn the value of staying in a trade and letting the value play out rather than jumping in to take profits too fast when your first set of datapoints are realized.

8. You can expect four to five good ideas per year. The rest turn out to be not so good, but it is important to go down multiple paths since you don't know which ones will come to fruition.

9. Don't worry too much about the downside. Take a variant view and keep doing the work. The risk of the variant view is also the opportunity. As the idea becomes consensus, the profitability declines but isn't entirely eliminated. It is important to be able to stay with the position over time.

10. Sell into strength as the rest of the investment community starts to recognize the story and your variant view is becoming consensus. That being said, recognize that over time there is value in holding on as a story unfolds even past the point where the idea becomes consensus, since even then there may still be considerable upside in the story. It is the same with shorts. You shouldn't rush to cover the first day a stock goes down.

11. In technology stocks, it costs more for research coverage, the variant view is cannibalized, and it is harder to get a unique view.

12. Part of the process of digging in deeper is communicating with people in the industry, reading financials, and making conference calls after you have formulated your own views and are looking for changes.

Build your own models, see earnings, and then compare your views to consensus so you can see how you differ from consensus. Keep looking for something that is not reflected in the estimates—a buyback, sale of another division, or a new management team.

13. It is often uncomfortable when your views diverge from the consensus, but this is where there is the most opportunity.

14. Do a probability analysis. Determine the theoretical expected value.

15. You want to mitigate risk in the sector and in the market, because there is infinite upside and defined downside. Remember that shorts are crowded, and there is a limited amount to borrow. You mitigate risk by hedging intelligently and by finding a basket of shorts that are somewhat negatively correlated with your longs.

The above illustrates what to me is a very well-defined and successful process for doing the kind of research necessary to find a unique, differentiated, and potentially profitable idea. Jeremy clearly developed a comparatively more elaborate process for putting on ideas and finding unique situations that would unlock the value of companies.

CASE STUDY ON HAVING A VARIANT PERCEPTION

Having a unique and differentiated idea is critical for succeeding in terms of goal achievement. But this goal-setting must be defined in terms of specific trading metrics, such as having a favorable winning percentage of trades (ideally 60 percent winners) and a positive W/L or slugging ratio (the average amount of money made on winning trades divided by the average amount of money lost on losing trades).

In order to do this, it is essential to set specific targets, breaking the overall goal into monthly, weekly, and even daily targets. As you break down your target, you have to figure out what is needed to reach it. If you are typically making X amount of money, what specifically can you do to increase that amount? Unfortunately, most people are not structured to achieve these kinds of higher rates of return. Listen in as I discuss these issues with Donald, a top-flight hedge fund manager who articulates these issues with clarity.

Donald: My goal in portfolio management is not to be the smartest or the most knowledgeable guy. It is to make money.... The key to this is to ensure that my daily actions and the decisions I am making about timing and the sizing of positions correspond with my goals. Most of the time, people just throw together a portfolio, and the rate of return at the end of the year is an output. They weren't really trying to manage a specific rate of return. The key to goal-setting is to decide on a specific target. I decide I am going to make X, but I can't put any restrictions on the idea. It can't be, "I am going to make X, but if the market is not good I am going to make fifty percent of X. If I can't find good ideas, I am going to make thirty." If the goal is going to be X, I have to figure out how I am going to get there regardless. I have to figure out a way to make X. I have to be able to say: "Here is my goal, and I am going to do whatever I can to get to that goal."

The whole notion is one of being uncomfortable, of pushing yourself, and that's how you ultimately wind up earning outsized rates of returns. You have to look at what the expectations are for the return of your capital. For my team, our goal, our sort of base case, is a thirty percent rate of return.

We focus on the rate of return on individual ideas. This is a fairly unique process that I have not encountered among very many people in the industry. What kind of rate of return do you need to have over the course of a year? It goes back to the end of the year. You say, "I really would like to make twenty or twenty-five or thirty percent"—whatever target you decide to set and to which you are willing to commit. Then you figure out how many ideas you need and how much you have to make in each one over specific periods of time to produce that end result. How many times do you come up with an idea and you still have to make twenty-five percent on the same year? If it's a good position, it's worth committing capital there. Calculate how much you are going to make on your winners on an annualized basis and how much are you going to lose on the average losers. The second thing is to consider how many of your ideas will be winners and how many will be losers. If you have sixty percent winners and forty percent losers, that would be very commendable.

Kiev: Could you distinguish between batting average and slugging ratio?

D: Sure. If you are a batter who gets only one out of four right every time you are at the plate, but every time you get it right you get a grand slam, you will have a high slugging percentage. There is a trade-off between batting average and slugging percentage. The more risk you want to take, the odds are you are going to have a higher slugging ratio but a lower batting average. On the other hand, if you just try to hit lots of singles, you are going to have a really high batting average, but your slugging percentage is not going to be very high. You can actually back into what kind of rate of return you should expect from your portfolio. If you use a sixty/forty and a one-and-a-half-to-one for the slugging ratio, you would need a thirty-seven-and-a-half percent return on your capital or gross market value. Now, let's assume you have to run hedged or dollar-neutral. You could be a little bit longer than that. You now need a seventy-five percent annualized rate of return when you're long winner in order to wind up with twelve-and-a-half percent return in gross exposure. It's an interesting exercise. By and large, people say, "It's a great idea for next year. I think I can make thirty, forty, or fifty percent on it," but when you really cut through it, the probability of being right versus wrong and what they make on their winners versus losers, they generally can't get to an acceptable rate of return in a portfolio. The way that people compensate for that is by taking big directional concentrated bets.

K: It sounds as if most people are not structured to achieve higher rates of return. How do you consider the possibility that your ideas may not give you the high rate of returns that you are looking for at the end of the year?

D: In my example, you want to make twelve-and-a-half percent on your gross, sixty/forty, one-and-a-half to one. To do this, you need to make thirty-seven-and-a-half percent on your GMV or zero on your shorts and seventy-five percent on your longs. In order to do this, you have to factor in the solution of time. So what if instead of having to make thirty-seven-and-a-half percent of GMV over the course of the year, you could start to trade your capital and look for opportunities where you could make profits in an average holding period of a *quarter*? So one-quarter of thirty-seven-and-a-half percent would be nine-point-four percent. You say "Wow!" All of a sudden, your opportunity for ideas just went up. Instead of looking for ideas that can make thirty-seven-and-a-half percent or seventy-five percent, now it's nine percent and eighteen percent. You say, "I think I could find a lot of ideas that could make eighteen percent over the course of a quarter."

Why is this relevant? Because if you are going to set what I would say is an acceptable target, then to look at it on an annualized basis you are just not going to get it. You are just not going to find enough ideas. But the map does work if you reduce your holding period and increase your idea velocity. Instead of taking a dollar capital and putting it to work and taking it back out at the end of the year, you put it to work and take it out at the end of the quarter and put it to work somewhere else.

K: All of a sudden, you have introduced the idea of turning your capital over to maximize profitability and achieve your goal at the end of the year.

D: It's not unlike blackjack. You can get a sense of how many face cards are left. So you can know whether their count is positive or negative. When the count is positive, your incentive is to bet as frequently as you can. You know how much you can use. Whenever you have a positive expected value, you want to keep betting. I am just trying to demystify why some traders are able to earn such high rates of returns. The first thing the best traders do is to set this great goal. The second thing is to ensure that idea velocity is unparalleled by having ideas submitted to a central portfolio from PMs and analysts throughout your firm. So you are always able to find something good.

The master trader knows that over time he is going to win sixty percent of the time. So the more times he can put his capital to work and take it back out, the higher the idea velocity and the higher the rate of return. He is able to put up his really high rates of return to articulate his capital risk.

Another approach is where you have an idea you love as a one percent position. Then the timing is optimal, and you take it to ten percent. This is another way you can create a rate of return through optimal sizing.

K: Most people think it's all about finding good ideas. If you have a good portfolio of good ideas, you will have the right outcomes. What do you think of that?

D: That's ignorant, because a lot of things can change between when you put that idea on and when your thesis is going to play out. The information you know today, the thesis you have today, deteriorates over time. Are the new variables built into the equation? If I buy this stock over time, am I going to be proven right? Maybe, maybe not. But if you have already resigned yourself to that over time, you're going to generate another idea.

K: Can you go over how this works in actual practice?

D: The thing that is really useful is this notion of setting a goal and having decisions about how you are sizing individual positions, the types of portfolio exposure that you have taken. How do your decisions explicitly relate to the goal? You know your capital base. You find out what the acceptable rate of return is. You are going to have a P-and-L dollar amount now. If you have a hundred million dollars, you want to make twelve-and-a-half percent on gross. So you need to make twelve-and-a-half million dollars. Once you have set that dollar goal, then when you are looking at an idea you can think, "What's my upside/downside? How many dollars do I want to try to make out of this idea?" If you say your idea is a percent of the portfolio, you say this is a "five percent idea." That doesn't address the fact that five percent in Company A is very different from five percent in Company B. You're starting the position from a percentage basis. It's actually nonsensical. The expected value of every one of those bets is different. So, if Company A has an expected value in your mind of ten percent, and you know Company B has two percent, why would you size them both at five? You really need to make Company B five times the size of Company A to have a similarly related expressed bet in terms of your conviction, what you think the expected value is. Next you have to determine the upside and the downside and the chances of being proven right or wrong.

K: If your objective is twelve-and-a-half percent, how much do you need to make in your best ideas if you are managing one hundred million dollars?

D: You probably need to make two or three million dollars. So, if you want to make three million dollars or two points, you have to be longer than a million-and-a-half shares. You need to be long a million-and-a-half shares to make three million dollars so you can get to your twelve-million-dollar goal. Now, does a million-and-a-half shares mean that the position is five percent, ten, twelve, fourteen, or eighteen? I don't know. That's the output. I can tell you unequivocally if you said, "I want to size this at five percent. It's my best idea." You know a five percent position goes from eight to twelve. That's two-hundred-and-fifty basis points in portfolio performance. Actually, since no one lets you run that long, you have to count on the fact that your hedge counts against your gross. Your bet is not your long. Your bet is the capital you need to commit to that. What I am trying to articulate for you is how you can take a P-and-L dollar goal based on the percent of capital and translate that into how you should be sizing your positions in terms of your goals. You can say, "On the top ideas I want to make three million dollars. On very good ideas I want to make seven-fifty. On my okay ideas I want to make three hundred." You have to find what is the top idea for you. On the very best ideas, you want to be right seven-and-a-half times out of ten. I want to have a slugging ratio of three to one.

K: How do you factor time into the equation?

D: We normalize our calculations to what we call time-adjusted expected value. So take the rate of return and annualize it by the time adjusted with the probability bets so that we can compare an idea that has a one-month view versus a one-year view. The purpose of it is to not set goals that are comfortable. You want to set stretch goals, and then you have to figure out how to handle them. You have to acknowledge that whatever you think today about an idea will change. You are just moving across the timeline investment. There is price up or down, and there is new information. Those three things are constantly tapped into risk/reward. So, once you have made decisions, you still have to reevaluate.

K: Any suggestions about tracking performance as it relates to goals?

D: You should have a spreadsheet of every position. What your target is, what you think you're going to get paid, a couple of lines on what your thesis is, and how many dollars you are trying to make out of the idea. You should have that to remind you and keep you honest. Once you have put it in there, you still have to have eyes and ears open. You still have to acknowledge if it's changing. Just because you have a twelve-dollar target and a stock goes from eight to seven, it doesn't mean it's a better idea now. You have to recalibrate everything in the whole thought process. That intellectual honesty is critical. No one is going to stand over you and ask whether you are being intellectually honest. If everything works, you can do it yourself and ultimately expect it from the people you are managing.

It's also useful to identify when you think you are going to get paid. The simplest answer is always on a quarterly earnings hit or miss, which is hard to predict, which is why we rarely do those kinds of trades because they just get crowded. I want to be in situations where I have an unambiguous answer to the question, "If I am right on a thesis, are we going to get paid on the stock?" I don't want to get into a situation where we are right on numbers, and we are long in a stock, and everyone else was leaning the same way that we were. For that reason, we are always looking for transformational stories such that you could say that a certain change would have an unambiguous effect on how people are going to perceive the security.

The other thing that we really hammer on people is the concept of returns on time invested. If you know that your goal of the portfolio is twelve million dollars, don't spend a lot of time on a position that you will never be able to get your arms around. Just acknowledge and say when you have done enough work to know that you are not going to be able to get comfortable with the idea.

The reason why that return of time invested is so critical is that you are so dependent on idea velocity. If you don't have five ideas, you had better be right all the time, and you had better make a lot on your winners relative to your losers. Otherwise, you are going to have to put up a bigger rate of return.

By developing a variant perception and defining this kind of path to getting paid, you can overcome any personality tendencies which may operate to hinder you from maximizing your performance. In this regard, it is useful to understand how you approach the research and goal-setting tasks and then work to understand the desirability of the particular models we have just explored, understanding what it is in your personality that may be impinging on how you can maximize your performance.

PERSONALITY FACTORS AND GOAL-SETTING

Remember, as a trading coach I am not interested in trying to change anyone's personality. I am somewhat skeptical as to whether people can in fact change that much even when they are motivated to change. But, I believe people can learn the way in which they are hardwired so that they can understand a bit better why they are acting and reacting the way they are, how they can compensate for some of those negative characteristics, and how they can exploit or maximize the use of their natural strengths in the performance process. If they can get some consciousness about themselves, they can move their game to an entirely new level.

Let me expand on this a bit more in terms of a few different traders and how their own personality factors influenced the way they were trading. I will then discuss some generic principles that one master hedge fund manager looks for and examine in greater detail some of the personality factors that color or influence the way in which a few more PMs function by way of understanding the complexity of the process.

Establishing a goal can sometimes be tricky, especially when you factor personalities into the equation. A *cautious or fearful* trader, for instance, may be reluctant to establish a goal that he considers too risky. For example, Mike had a difficult start to the year but had finally come out on top. He made $7.5 million the previous month and was up about $18 million for the year. Because of his success, he needed to set a new goal. He was thinking about $2 million per month over the next three months. When pushed to set a total goal of $25 million for the year, however, he balked, saying that the extra $1 million might be too much of a stretch. When I pushed the issue, he said that he didn't think he could find more ideas, but he could scale up in a paired way with more capital. In order to make the goal work for him, Mike has to overcome his limited aspirations. Currently he is content to make a few million dollars per year. This is probably a result of the fact that he came from a poor, rural upbringing and has a very cautious, conservative, long-only background at his previous place of employment. Whereas his statistics are such that there *is* room to take such a bet, it is not clear whether he is comfortable doing what it takes to do so. So even though Mike expresses interest in getting bigger and taking more directional risk, it may take a while—using baby steps instead of leaps.

Another trader, Dylan, is budgeted for $30 million, but he is expecting to make $100 million and has about $80 million built into his forecasts for the positions he is following. He actually expects to find one stock that will net him $100 million. I asked him why he was limiting himself to one position instead of looking for two or three. Dylan needed to consider that a stretch target would lead him to do more work and tap more of his resources. He came up with $150 million as a stretch target and seemed genuinely empowered by this concept.

Instead of fearful or cautious, other traders may be *overzealous, extremely optimistic, or even a bit arrogant*. This might lead them to aim too high, establishing goals that are unrealistic or out of reach. For example, Gerald set a $500,000-per-month goal but was able to reach only about $250,000. After careful consideration, he found that his target was too aggressive. He lowered his goal to $250,000 with the expectation that when he reaches that amount consistently he can raise the bar a little at a time.

Insecurity is another personality trait that may prevent traders from reaching ultimate success. For instance, Brandon is an *insecure* trader who is a bit overwhelmed by his experiences of the past year. He experienced a few misses and tends to approach new positions with a lack of confidence. Further review suggested that he doesn't have a plan or strategy and that he pursues new ideas somewhat randomly without any differentiated approach to building levels of conviction and high-grading his ideas.

We talked about developing a specific goal-oriented strategy. He wants to do 20 percent of his own $200 million and 20 percent in another $300 million portfolio. In order to do this, he needs to start thinking of how many high-conviction (where he can take 10 percent) and medium-conviction (where he can take 7 percent) ideas he needs to develop for the year. He also needs to consider the probabilistic price action in the stocks and what other kinds of work he will have to do. He needs to improve the efficiency of his efforts, perhaps cutting back on ideas that are impossible to get datapoints for, and needs to spend some time on finding stocks that have a longer horizon until fruition.

These examples illustrate how personality factors can influence the way in which people approach goals. In my experience, the approaches outlined in this book provide a methodology that can be applied by a variety of individuals, irrespective of their personalities. Indeed, I would go so far as to say that the goal-oriented approach helps individuals to bypass their individual idiosyncrasies and begin to trade in terms of a larger and sounder methodology.

If you can learn these approaches and then learn the requisite work needed to generate ideas, you can indeed learn how to trade successfully with the trader's edge quite independently of your personality proclivities. So even if you are impulsive or cautious, or fearful or perfectionistic, it is possible to adapt this kind of goal-oriented methodology.

RECOGNIZING GOAL-DIRECTED INDIVIDUALS

Goal-directed individuals, or those traders who use targets to direct their efforts, will often demonstrate distinct personality traits. For instance, a goal-directed trader is often considered an *achiever*. He exhibits an almost insatiable drive to achieve something every day—including weekends and holidays. If he isn't achieving, he isn't satisfied. This internal fire pushes him to do more and provides energy to keep persevering without burning out.

These types of individuals are also tagged as *focused*. They have the ability to set a goal and doggedly stay on task, and this ability helps them filter out irrelevancies and to determine which actions will help them achieve their goals. Of course, there is a downside to this kind of determination in that these individuals are often impatient with delays and obstacles and frequently dissatisfied with their own progress.

Candidates who are goal-directed are also *avid learners*. They are energized by steady and deliberate journeys from ignorance in a particular area to competence. They thrive in dynamic work environments where they are expected to learn a lot about a new subject in a short period of time. Whereas this personality characteristic lends itself to goal-directedness, surprisingly, individuals like this can also have trouble actually achieving the result because they continue to delve deeper to learn more and fail to see the point at which it is beneficial to move on.

Some goal-directed individuals also demonstrate what Prussian military strategist Karl von Clausewitz called the *coup d'oeil*, the intuitive ability to grasp the essence of things at a glance or to objectively see the whole picture. An individual with this characteristic is more likely to keep his cool and then make the correct decisive moves. He is in a constant race to find new strategies that have not yet been discovered by his competition.

Listen to what one fund manager says about the kinds of people he looks for when hiring for his $7 billion firm:

> *We look at whether the guy played team sports. I prefer team sports to individual. He needs to have some longevity and love of the game. Was he a leader? Did he take a job that illustrates he has the desire to learn? Has he demonstrated the ability to do something that broadens his horizon? How does he carry himself? We look at all those factors. We ask him how he measures his professional success five years from now. We are also screening for the likeability quotient and for work ethic. I like people who have been knocked down a little bit. We ask, "What are three things you expect as a player? How do you judge your own success in five to ten years? What makes you tick?" I like to ask people about the hardest thing they have ever done. So when people say, "I have failed" and take responsibility for it, I like that answer over the answer that blames the environment.*

So, when you are interviewing a potential portfolio manager, remember that you are trying to gauge how conscious he has been, how designing of his own career path. Does he make things happen? Is he a maximizer, an opportunist, someone who is proactive about his career? Consider asking the following questions:

- How much has your career been governed or guided by a plan? Give two examples.
- What is your P&L target? Specify this in terms of your trading/ investment time horizon for the year, month, week, and/or day. Have you ever considered longer-term goals? Do you have a three-year or a five-year plan?
- What is your strategy for producing these results? How do you plan to reach your target? What is your strategy for building your portfolio? How do you intend to size your positions? What are your thoughts about sizing positions in terms of level of conviction (low, medium, and high conviction)?
- What are the catalysts that you are looking for and other factors on the path to getting paid?

- What factors in the marketplace, company calls, and other information would lead you to reduce your position? What factors would lead you to enlarge your position?
- What plan do you have to manage your losses? Have you thought about a stop-loss?
- What are the two most adverse experiences you have ever faced? How did you handle those experiences? How do you handle drawdowns or difficult situations in the marketplace?
- Do you have the discipline to stay true to your commitments? What more do you need to do to increase your commitment?

Remember, you are looking for indicators that the candidate not only knows how to set a goal but that he consciously establishes targets and develops plans to reach those targets, that he is not easily distracted from his goals, and that he has an ability to turn a lemon into lemonade—to grow from adversity. You want to discern his desire for personal challenge, his growth potential. Ask him to give specific examples of his past experiences to try to estimate how he will do in the future.

A critical point to remember in assessing goal-directedness is that this set of behavioral patterns does not appear in a vacuum. It is generally part and parcel of a variety of behavioral characteristics that together constitute the overall personality of an individual. Moreover, given the impact of other personality qualities, goal-directedness is never a single variable but the complex result of the interaction of many different variables.

So, it is important when evaluating someone to consider the kinds of things that are most relevant to the task at hand, general principles that are relevant across the board to success in a variety of performance endeavors. Then you need to understand how various traits interact with each other to create the final mix that is reflected in the unique configuration presented by an individual. In looking at goal-directedness, you want to understand the quantity and quality of the traits and the associated personality characteristics that might influence how he approaches goals, how receptive he is to coaching, and how flexible and adaptive he is to new information.

For example, some people may want to be coached in the process of establishing a goal. Some may pay attention to the rules and procedures of the larger organization. Others are inclined to be governed by their own internal compasses and may even bristle at the constraints placed on them by the larger organization. Others may want to do things on their own. Some traders approach goals perfectionistically, with a great sense of thoroughness and caution; others are dominated by a great sense of urgency and establish goals in a risky and less cautious way.

CASE STUDY ON RECOGNIZING GOAL-DIRECTEDNESS

Whether you are looking for new hires or trying to help move your current employees (or yourself) toward greater avenues of success, you must recognize that people approach goals differently. The more you can understand their underlying personality dynamics, the more you will understand how they function in the goal-setting environment and how they interact with their challenges, their teammates, with management, and others, how they handle stress, how they respond to setbacks, drawdowns, and criticism, and what you can expect in terms of working with them.

To give you an example of how to do this, let's consider Fred, a 30-year-old portfolio manager who is very smart and talented. Fred has a number of years of experience working in merger arbitrage in a large banking institution and is now functioning as a portfolio manager in a large hedge fund. Let's explore a composite of his strengths and weaknesses. As you read through the information, look at each characteristic through the frame of goal-directedness.

Fred's Strengths: The Three *C*s

1. Confident
2. Competitive
3. Persuasive communicator

Confident Fred is very confident in his abilities and desires to work alone, without a high degree of supervision. He functions best on tasks that allow him to develop and implement plans that clearly establish outcomes and performance but leave the actual methods undefined. Because Fred likes to make choices, he is more of an action-oriented person and therefore knows how to quickly implement decisions. He will not be happy trying to fit into a structure created by someone else. He would probably be better off building his own team within a larger organization where he has a fair degree of autonomy.

Competitive   Fred is also highly competitive and motivated by his desire to excel. He can be expected to work hard and to outdo others and would do well in an environment where he can be acknowledged for his efforts and his ability to outshine his contemporaries. He is motivated by contests or activities in which there is an incentive offered—commissions, bonuses, prizes, and publicized status. Because of this, he performs well in environments in which individual productivity and performance is measured and compared to his own prior performance and/or the performance of others.

Persuasive Communicator   Fred is a very persuasive and assertive and frequently dominates conversations. He is outspoken and transparent and not afraid of what others think about him. As such, he isn't afraid to give his opinions or provide advice and actually enjoys the opportunity to convince others to accept his point of view, even if they are reluctant to do so. Fred welcomes the opportunity to overcome resistance and build support. Given this, he doesn't become easily flustered when he faces conflict or stressful interpersonal challenges. He takes negative events in stride.

Assessment   Confidence, persuasive communication, and competitiveness come through in Fred's approach to goals. This is the way in which he functions, but it doesn't necessarily tell us how effective he will be in pursuing and achieving the goals that he sets. These goals relate more to stylistic patterns that emerge from observing him. Certainly he is confident, competitive, and a good debater, but goal-orientation implies a little more. It implies that he is able to follow a disciplined methodology and process. Indeed, when we look further at Fred's personality profile we find a few weaknesses that must balance our understanding of his personality in order to see how best to guide him in his efforts to achieve his goals.

There are some areas that are inhibiting Fred from moving forward with his career. As you continue to read, you may notice a direct correlation between Fred's strengths and his weaknesses. In fact, as with most of our personalities, there is a flipside to our positive characteristics that can actually inhibit us. However, if we recognize these problems we can view them as opportunities to better ourselves.

Fred's Weaknesses: The Three *I*s

1. Intolerant of details
2. Independent-minded
3. Easily interrupted

Intolerant of Details Whereas Fred is action-oriented and self-motivated, he also fails to pay attention to the details. So, he needs to develop the self-discipline to examine the results with an eye toward catching mistakes. If he perceives a problem, he needs to stick with it until it has been corrected. Then, he needs to slow down, check and recheck the facts and figures, and make sure he has met established standards and delivered on all his commitments to others. Basically, Fred needs to see tasks through to completion without overlooking important steps along the way, to be efficient without sacrificing accuracy.

Independent-Minded Fred's independent nature is a good thing, but because he doesn't seek the approval of others, he may not be perceived as being team-oriented. In addition, because Fred is not afraid to speak his mind, he can often push teammates further away instead of working out a compromise. He needs to learn how to work toward a common ground when he meets with resistance and to pick his battles. In addition, he needs to learn how to share his expertise and extend himself to others in an effort to enhance the team's performance. He also has to learn how to be patient when others communicate differently and to listen with the intent to understand rather than with the intent to reply.

Easily Interrupted Fred has a habit of allowing distractions to unnecessarily slow him down. Therefore, he needs to learn how to view interruptions in a controlled manner, separating the immediate from the critical. One practical way he can do this is to put at least a brief amount of time between a new request and his response. This will give him the time he needs to come to an appropriate solution without needlessly interrupting his schedule. In order to manage his priorities more efficiently, it may be important to break down larger projects into manageable components.

Assessment Fred is a smart, talented individual with a great drive for autonomy and competition and a need to dominate those around him. All these things work fine in terms of goal-setting, but his lack of patience and tolerance, and the fact that he gets bored easily and does not like focusing on details, mean that to achieve the kinds of results that he wants he needs to find additional support to complement his strengths. He needs some analysts who are thorough, cautious, and very careful who can do the detailed work necessary to run a large portfolio. At the same time, he probably needs to spend some time developing a greater capacity for listening to and coaching others so that he can bring his hires up to speed.

Could Fred become a detail person? That is probably not likely, but with his strong, outspoken nature he could easily become a successful team leader once he bites the bullet and recognizes that he needs more of this careful kind of work to assist him in pursuing his goals.

GOAL-DIRECTEDNESS IN TURBULENT TIMES

Of course, wherever there is a goal, there is the possibility of wandering away from it, and that is often a reality for even the most goal-directed individual. As I have conducted a number of coaching conversations with individual portfolio managers, I have witnessed a variety of patterns demonstrating how individuals veer from the goal-directed target. Every person is unique and a variety of personality characteristics as well as previous life experiences contribute to the way in which any individual responds to turbulent times. Traders are no different. Some seem more resilient and able to recover from drawbacks and failures; others seem to languish and even give up at the slightest change in fortune.

Consider the months of July and August 2007. The subprime mortgage debacle significantly impacted the credit markets and then began to spill over into emerging markets. Ryan went back to the drawing board. He took advantage of the opportunity to prepare for the future with fundamental analysis and used this period of time to reduce his risk and to do scenario analysis and look for displacements and opportunities and short-term trading opportunities while building his fundamental ideas.

Ian, on the other hand, became overwhelmed by the situation. He felt stuck in a panic mode, like a deer in the headlights. He attributed his drawdown during this period to the fact that he, like everyone else, had been caught in the same trades, and it was difficult to get out of positions during the deleveraging phase since the shorts kept going up and the longs kept going down. He said that as he got out of good stocks to provide more liquidity, he was whipsawed on the short side. What he didn't do was regroup, try to correct his errors, and make a plan for the future. Instead, he whined about his losses and licked his wounds.

The sign of a truly goal-oriented individual is that in times of great stress he gives an increased effort at trying to understand all the forces at work and begins planning for a variety of future scenarios so that he is well prepared to take advantage of opportunities when the market begins to turn. Ryan demonstrated this ability. Ian did not.

Another trader, Ric, handled the same market in a different way. During March of the same year, he had learned to get out in the early phases of a drawdown and therefore reduced his capital outlay to 60 percent so that he could weather the storm better. This wasn't comfortable to do and it took some discipline to fight what he described as his own "greedy impulses" to hold on. But this self-awareness helped a lot, and he was able to avoid a massive drawdown during a period when other PMs in his space were being severely hurt.

Although there are as many reactions as there are traders for any set of circumstances, let's consider some very specific suggestions on reacting positively in turbulent markets and how your reactions relate to goal-directedness.

Own Your Stuff

Like Ian, many traders fail to take responsibility for their mistakes or for their failures to continue on the path toward their goals. They become preoccupied with what others are doing and seem unable to "own their stuff." Tristan, for example, was concerned about his $4 million drawdown. Instead of recognizing his own failure to get the trades right, he is still wondering how others are doing and what the firm's policy is about letting people go. While he believes he should cut down further, he is failing to prepare for future scenarios even though he thinks the market may be presenting a unique buying opportunity at this time. Given his preoccupation with everyone else, Tristan will not be prepared to take on risk when things settle down because he won't have taken time to figure out where the opportunities will be.

Review the Game Films

How do you know what went wrong and what went right unless you review the events? Just like coaches often review game films to find out what needs to be tweaked before the next big game, traders must learn to look back on their decisions to see what could have been changed that might have created a more favorable outcome. Jake deleveraged from $3.1 billion to under $2 billion and took net market value (NMV) down to about 12 percent. Still he felt that there was much unwinding and that things wouldn't stabilize until later in the year. He learned a lot of lessons from his experiences—one of them being that some of the senior analysts, especially covering European stocks, probably had too much discretion and not enough risk experience for handling the drawdown. He felt that too much authority was delegated to them and is encouraging changes in the structuring of his firm as a result.

Switch Gears?

Of course, once a trader has reviewed his actions and reactions and determined what could have been done differently, he may discover that some very serious changes need to be made, not only in the structures around him, but also in terms of his strategy for reaching his goal. Sometimes traders have to learn to articulate new strategies that take advantage of the changed financial climate. Sometimes traders have to rethink their risk management strategies in terms of responding appropriately to the market and finding new opportunities in the market in light of the market's changed risk profile.

For example, sometimes too much of the profits are generated on the long side. So when the market environment changes, some PMs don't know what to do. No one wants to sell their longs and many are uncomfortable shorting stocks or at least hedging their portfolio. Traders need to learn to be more transparent about their plans regarding capital cuts. Often PMs aren't as resistant to capital cuts as might be expected as long as they are given the opportunity to discuss and understand the circumstances.

Be Realistic

When a trader experiences a significant setback, he needs to consider whether his current goal was ever realistic. Sometimes in the excitement of setting goals, traders get carried away and fail to look at the reality of their current situation: their available capital, current market conditions, and their risk parameters. A successful trader will define more realistic expectations going forward and reformulate his goals in terms of monthly targets and try sticking with an already-proven process.

Stay True to Your Strengths

Another way in which a trader can handle turbulent times and still stay on course (or get back on course) is to identify the sources of loss that are secondary to not following his strongest suit. In other words, he takes the opportunity to see where he has veered away from his strengths. Sam was losing money in small-sized positions in stocks where he had some edge but not the highest conviction. When he began to think about it, he realized that this seemed to be a repetitive pattern. In addition, after he reviewed some of his losses relative to the holding period, he realized that there were some stocks in which he lost money three months in a row. He is obviously not playing to his strengths and is going to monitor this more carefully going forward.

Sam was busy trying to test out a variety of strategies suggested by other people and was not concentrating on digging deeper into the companies that he knew in the specific sector of his expertise. As he began to focus and concentrate on utilizing his own strengths, he began to perform at a considerably higher rate of success than in the past. The key was getting him to shift his thinking from that of a student to that of an expert in the kind of technology companies that he knew and understood from his days in private equity.

Maintain Focus

Perhaps the most important way a trader can stay goal-directed even in the face of a drawdown is to stay focused. He must be resilient and aware of his impulses and how they may be influencing his trading. He can't just pretend to be tough. He has to focus on his goal and how he can get to it, even when things aren't going his way. There is increased suggestibility at times of increased market pressure. So, a goal-directed trader will be more alert to these kinds of things and pay attention to the possibility that he is being influenced by the defensive attitudes of others.

In addition to these steps that individuals can take during difficult markets, there are also firm-wide adjustments that can be made to help traders stay goal-directed during turbulent times. For instance, firms can:

- Encourage teamwork.
- Reduce GMV.
- Change the market paradigm.
- Make specific suggestions to traders on handling market volatility.
- Ask traders what can be done to help them.
- Impose penalties for people who don't cut their GMV when requested.
- Provide incentives for traders who find ways to make more money.

- Help traders recognize when to get back into the market.
- Maintain open communication between management and traders.
- Delever portfolios in time of crisis.

The gist of these various recommendations pertains to ways of reducing risk by getting rid of low-conviction ideas, increasing the amount of work done in high-conviction ideas, reducing the amount of capital being used (deleveraging) until such time as the markets become more rational, and functioning more in terms of fundamental analysis and less in terms of emotional turbulence created by worldwide confusion. Many of these suggestions are designed to improve communication, develop incentives for people functioning in more risk-controlled ways, and encourage traders to pay attention to the larger needs of the firm and not just their own portfolios. Turbulent times offer a chance for greater diligence, discipline, and managerial oversight until things settle down and there is a chance to return to the old ways of making money.

 CHAPTER IN REVIEW

1. A detailed trading plan, which includes a unique variant perception and the path to getting paid, will allow you to focus limited psychological energy more efficiently.

2. In order to set a realistic but challenging goal:
   - Review what you have done in the past.
   - See what is repeatable.
   - Consider the resources available to you.
   - Understand the firm's standards.
   - Divide your annual goal into monthly or weekly targets.

3. To become a master trader, you need to not only set a goal but do everything possible to ensure that you reach that goal.

4. If you are insecure, cautious, fearful, overconfident, or even arrogant, developing a variant perception and defining a path to getting paid can help you overcome personality tendencies that may operate to hinder you from achieving maximum performance.

5. Whereas goal-directed individuals are often known as achievers, focused, avid learners, and extremely self-controlled individuals, to be a truly

goal-oriented trader you need to make an increased effort during times of great stress.

6. Try to understand all the forces at work and plan for a variety of future scenarios so that you will be well prepared to take advantage of opportunities when the market begins to turn. Some ways in which you can do this are to:

   • Take responsibility for your own actions.

   • Analyze what went right and wrong in previous trades.

   • Be ready to switch gears when necessary.

   • Be realistic.

   • Capitalize on your strengths.

   • Stay focused.

7. Another way of formulating the goal setting conversation is as follows. In the context of goal setting, if you want to make 12 percent on gross market value then you have to do a lot better than that on your winning positions in order to offset your losing positions. If you are right 60 percent of the time (i.e., winning percentage of 60 percent) and you make 2x more on your winners than you lose on your losers (i.e., Win/Loss Ratio) then in order to make 12 percent you need to make 30 percent on your winners and lose 15 percent on your losers.

$$(30\% \times .6) - (15\% \times .4) = 12\%$$

To place 30 percent in context, since this is on gross market value then your long needs to outperform your short by 60 percent (60% / 2 = 30%) on an annualized basis.

The point is that 60 percent is a large number, which helps explain why generating returns is difficult and more specifically, why finding ideas with one-year horizons doing 60 percent is a less effective way than finding ideas with a three-month horizon doing 15 percent but finding 4x as many.

CHAPTER 3

"Fire in the Belly"

The Ability to Take Appropriate Risk

C ompetitiveness is what former MLB general manager Frank Cashen called "fire in the belly." Competitiveness is that burning, inner need to win—not simply winning the game, but to win with every move the player makes on the ice/court/field. The competitive individual wants to score, wants to assist, and in short, wants to do everything possible to beat the opposing player as a key means of gaining personal gratification. It is somewhat separate from aggressiveness in that aggressiveness is simply the desire to hit. Competitiveness is the overall desire to win—to win with skill and/or to win with aggressiveness. In trading, competitiveness and risk-taking are two traits that go hand-in-hand. Truly competitive traders realize that in order to win they have to manage risk successfully.

A PICTURE OF SUCCESSFUL RISK MANAGEMENT

Risk-taking is about a willingness to enter into the unknown, to take a bet based on insufficient information in an unpredictable market. Successful risk-taking behavior is the ability to take risk in a controlled way, follow the rules, manage drawdowns, cull losers, add to winners, express conviction in ideas in terms of sizing, and use capital appropriately. Most portfolio managers have the capacity to do this, but there is a range from those who are very thorough and cautious to those who are swashbucklers. Some people are not compliant and need to be better controlled by persuasion; some people are risk averse and need to be encouraged to use more capital; some people are not adequately hedged and not risk-controlled enough. Some people hold onto losers too long. Others don't hold their winners long enough. Others look for an edge in little-known or -followed stocks (e.g., microcap stocks or small-cap stocks). These give them an edge but present liquidity problems such that if there are problematic or stress events in the market they cannot get out of their illiquid positions—not a good way to manage risk.

The successful trader, though, is a goal-oriented risk-taker with good abstract reasoning and not too much of the cautiousness or thoroughness that might interfere with his ability to trade stocks in his portfolio. The person's risk profile may be more cautious and thorough if he is going to be a long-term value investor. In that case, his cautiousness and thoroughness may support the kind of portfolio strategy he has developed to do very thorough work, to buy stocks when they are cheap and to hold them for long periods of time as they mature in value.

The best risk-takers are able to run balanced books, get bigger when they have an edge, and take risks in calculated ways. I look for people that are willing to take measured risk in their lives and are not so cautious and such perfectionists that they cannot pull the trigger. For example, successful traders know how to:

- Control downside risk and manage drawdowns by reducing the size of positions during times of loss or when approaching drawdown territory.
- Control downside by managing hedged books where they are not too long or too short in the way they are managing positions.
- Get bigger in high-conviction ideas and express high conviction by sizing their bets, especially before catalysts or critical events in the marketplace.
- Stay out of illiquid positions that make it difficult to sell stocks that aren't working.

The following are some general guidelines to help you assess risk-taking ability when interviewing someone or when trying to improve your own risk-taking abilities. Consider each category and ask the questions that follow:

Trading Philosophy

You want to determine how conscious this trader has been in the creation of his career. Is he designing? Does he make things happen? Is he a maximizer or an opportunist? What motivates this trader? Is he aware of what motivates him? How flexible or how rigid is he? Can he adapt to various circumstances? Some of these things can be discerned from his career history as well as from his own formulation of his career. Ask the following questions to gain more information:

- What are your goals, strategy, outperformance targets, longer-term plans?
- How much has your career been governed or guided by a plan?
- Do you consider yourself achievement oriented?
- What motivates you?
- Can you give an example of pushing the envelope or stretching the boundaries in terms of generating ideas or in a personal activity?
- What would it take to motivate you?
- How do you motivate yourself?

Handling Drawdowns

In order to gauge a trader's potential success, you must first know how he handles failure. You need to know how he handles stress and adversity, as well as his resilience and capacity to recover. Is he able to pace himself? How often does he make mistakes? Is his life a series of catastrophes, and if so, how much was he responsible for these problems? Does he have the ability to grow from adversity, to become an even better trader after failure? Is he risk averse? In addition, you want to judge his appetite for risk and, therefore, his personal growth potential. You may be able to discern the answers to these questions by considering significant events in his life history. You also need to ask:

- What are the two most significant elements of adversity you have ever faced?
- How much and how did you grow as a result of such experiences?
- What have you learned, and how have you changed as a result of such experiences?
- What kinds of things derail you?

- How do you typically respond to adversity? For example, are you prone to sulk, complain, or get aggressive? Do you give up or work harder?
- Do you stick to your conviction in the face of negative market responses?
- Give an example of how you knew to hold on or when you knew to get out of a specific trade?
- What did you learn from that experience? (Follow through on this, because some traders don't learn from a negative market response.)
- How much are you distracted by your own emotions (such as greed, fear, envy, jealousy, paranoia, or depression)?

Head versus Heart

A successful trader is a unique mix of passion and dedication. His determination will create in him a desire to know more about his companies than anyone else in the world, but he will also rely on a certain amount of instincts that are the result of love for the job. Ask him:

- At what age did you begin to trade?
- Do you have a personal account?
- What attracts you to this job?
- What work do you do to ensure that you know your company better than anyone else?
- What makes your efforts unique?
- Can you give an example of how you used your gut instinct to make an important decision?
- How do you reconcile instinct and thought process in regard to decision making?

Although appropriate risk management is critical to successful trading, it is not a purely natural thing to do. In order to become a winning trader, a PM must be willing to review risk statistics with the risk manager so as to find ways of improving his overall performance, to examine personality factors that are likely to influence his risk management skills, and to explore various strategies that can upgrade his performance.

Reviewing Risk Statistics

A winning trader must be able to function in terms of outsized performance targets. By looking at a trader's profitability or P&L, his percentage of winning trades, his slugging ratio or W/L ratio, as well as his Sharpe ratio and other risk statistics from his previous job, it is possible to identify certain behavioral patterns that are reflective of his overall past performance (i.e., whether he doesn't take enough risk, takes too much, is not balanced, doesn't cull his losers, or doesn't get bigger in his winners). A lot of these factors are secondary to underlying psychological patterns, and from them you can make certain assumptions about future performance. If the individual has no prior track record, then it is important to review his life experiences for evidence of calculated risk-taking, goal-directedness, and the like. This, coupled with the use of psychological tests, can give you a sense of his or her ability to handle the uncertainties of the marketplace and deal with unpredictable events and insufficient information.

Of course, one of the most basic ways to assess a trader's ability to take risk is to examine his portfolio management. Although there is no unique way to structure a portfolio in terms of sizing, clearly, how it is structured is often reflective of the personality of the PM and therefore his ability to take risk.

Some PMs prefer to trade only a few, highly concentrated positions all the time (say between 5 percent to 15 percent of buying power [BP]). These portfolio managers are generally big risk-takers with a lot of confidence in their ability to trade and high conviction in their ideas. They tend to have large slugging ratios and outsized profits, but they also tend to exhibit lower Sharpe ratios and larger drawdowns.

The biggest danger for this style occurs when an overly confident and inexperienced portfolio manager doesn't reduce his position when the market says he is wrong and so suffers large drawdowns to the point of hitting his *down and out* (that amount of loss that triggers the dissolution of that manager's portfolio). This pattern often occurs among new and inexperienced portfolio managers who are trying to hit homeruns.

Another danger of this high-conviction portfolio style is the tendency to stick with losers. Most humans have the desire to prove themselves right. In some, that desire can lead to self-destruction. When some traders get in a hole, instead of getting out, recouping, and starting over, they hang on, even adding to losing positions in hope that their "luck" will change, that the position will turn around and they will recover. Unfortunately, the opposite is often the case. They wind up losing everything.

Take Cameron, for example. Cameron is known for closing out winners early and sticking with losers too long. In 2006, he was down $8 million—$6 million of which was attributable to one position. He made

$6 million in the position in the previous year and continued to believe it was a high-conviction idea in the next year despite the fact that the market didn't show its normal seasonality in early January even with positive data and good earnings. The company reported a decline in gross margins that knocked the price down, but Cameron didn't risk-manage the position or put in stops so as to preserve some of his profits from the previous year. The stock continued to decline in price, and he continued to hang on, eventually giving up all his profits. Even with his losses, Cameron admits that if he weren't down so much he would have been buying more.

Of course, a set of constraints should generally be established that PMs should be expected to follow. An example of one such set of constraints might be as follows: no more than 10 percent of the portfolio with more than 2 days of trading volume; 7 percent for 5 days; 5 percent for 10 days; and 2 percent for 20 days. This means that the PM should not have more than 10 percent of all his positions that take more than 2 days of trading volume to exit the position, and so on. This is not onerous, but some PMs experience it as such.

A case in point is Chris. Chris was running 50 names—most of them low-conviction ideas. He tended to focus on low illiquid-cap stocks that were barely covered by investment analysts at brokerage firms and investment banks. Managing illiquid stocks can be profitable if things move up but can be problematic if there are catastrophic events and the stocks plummet.

Chris had a large position in a small biotech company that he was selling. The path to getting paid was his expectation that it would be sold to a larger biotech company. The problem was that this position was illiquid, and illiquidity hurt Chris's ability to do something in other stocks. Chris noted that he had an edge in less-trafficked names because no one else knew about the stocks and he had an edge on the competition, but this created a risk for the firm. If too many PMs took this approach and got into too many illiquid positions, it would be difficult to deliver in the event of a catastrophe in the market, as happened in the summer of 2007 during the subprime mortgage and credit crunch debacle.

Another portfolio consideration to look for is the trader's drawdown control, a vital indication of whether the PM has good risk management techniques in place and is able to recognize when he is in drawdown and can take appropriate measures to reduce his losing positions and the chances of getting into even greater drawdown. This is an important portfolio management skill that PMs need to follow and demonstrate before anyone would want to give them more capital. It suggests discipline and good corporate citizenship. Most important, it means that the PM is not being run by his emotional responses, leading him to do foolish things such as double down when things aren't working. It is also important that the PM deliver before drawdown limits are reached, and in particular, not hold onto losers.

The following are some more basic considerations to examine within a trader's portfolio in order to get a better idea of how well a trader manages risk:

- **Long stocks only:** Does the PM have a lot of ideas on the short side? Does he hedge himself with equity indices on the short side to stay within his net market value (NMV) exposure limits? Is he implicitly making sector bets by employing a broad-based index hedge instead of finding not only long alpha plays but short alpha plays where no single-stock shorts can be identified? A good approach is a custom basket in his sector.
- **Poor alpha generation:** Performance should be viewed relative to the performance in his sector. Some portfolio managers may appear to be doing well when, in reality, a large portion of their P&L is simply generated when they are long and their sector has run strongly, not because of stock selection.
- **P/L distribution:** Sometimes returns are dominated by one or two positions for the entire year. This could be a problem if these one or two outsized P&L results are not repeatable year after year. A distribution of P&L where the magnitude of the top winners—trade by trade by trade—exceeds the magnitude of the top losers is preferable. This results in a P&L distribution that is skewed to the positive or right side and is an indication of a repeatable process and risk management style.

Of course, there are times when an individual doesn't have the specific career or life experiences to evaluate the above criteria. Then it becomes essential to evaluate them psychologically as well as in terms of their life histories.

Examining Personality Factors

Whereas an individual's past history can provide a clue as to how he is going to handle decision making in situations where he has insufficient information and how he is going to manage toward greater performance, his personality can also play a significant part in how he takes risk. If an individual is too cautious or too thorough or in a psychological sense too much of a perfectionist, he is likely to have difficulty in adapting to a goal-oriented, high-performance approach to portfolio management. In addition, it is important to screen out traders who are too impulsive, impatient, and perhaps irrational risk-takers who lack sufficient cautiousness and thoroughness to prevent them from blowing up.

In doing so, you must consider personality proclivities to determine whether they will be able to adapt to the challenging role of portfolio manager. It is also important to evaluate how they handle work assignments during a two-to-three-month evaluation period, when you can observe how they prepare, then report and respond to constructive criticism, as well as how they interact with members of your team. This type of evaluation will give you the best sense of how they are likely to do. One fund manager I know claims it takes him three years to really make up his mind as to whether someone will be ready for the long haul. The following are a few examples of different personality profiles to give you some idea of the kinds of considerations that are useful when evaluating an individual in terms of managing a portfolio.

The Stubborn Risk-Taker   Rebecca is an urgent risk-taker who may be a bit stubborn in her approach to risk-taking and not too coachable. She is a very self-assured trader who exhibits a forceful leadership style. While she is more than willing to challenge the status quo, she demonstrates a sense of urgency that may manifest in impatience with time on the job. Her stubborn nature may lead her to believe that her way is the best or only way of doing something, thus limiting her capacity to benefit from the suggestions that others bring. Moreover, as she tends to be rather skeptical of people's intentions, she could build walls that discourage a give-and-take relationship. Still, she is very calculated and responsible in her actions as well as very results oriented.

While she addresses issues immediately, if she has a particular plan in mind, she might not consider outside resources that could add to the richness of her recommendations. A born competitor, Rebecca displays the analytical ability to perform well in a portfolio management role. She is apt to seek out new and creative means to achieve strong returns and shows the decisiveness to take advantage of opportunities as soon as possible.

Philip is another stubborn, long-term value-oriented PM. He gets attached to ideas, especially illiquid ideas, and holds them too long. He doesn't follow good risk management principles. His winning trade percentage is 46 percent and basically not good across all holding periods. He has high-conviction ideas but seems to hold onto things out of belief even when they are going against him. Nevertheless, he has a high slugging ratio (the amount of profit he makes in his winning trades over the amount he loses in his losing trades) and obviously understands his stocks in some big, macro way.

Unfortunately, he tends not to be able to grasp the message of risk. He is holding good ideas too long and keeps holding them as they go down in value, giving back much of the profit he has made. His tendency to hold on a long time to losers is reflective of high conviction but not good risk management. His extreme illiquidity (being in stocks that take several days to liquidate because they don't trade that many shares a day) puts his portfolio at great risk. Some of his biggest trades will take 15, 25, and 40 days to liquidate, which could be disastrous for him and for the firm if there were a catastrophic event. He was unable to define a timeframe and delineation of the path to getting paid for many of his stocks in terms of specific catalysts, which would help give him more conviction and enable him to build up in size. Traders like Phillip may hold onto losers too long, getting themselves into a deeper drawdown because of an unrealistic hope that things will turn around.

The Reserved Risk-Taker Some traders fail to utilize all their buying power and don't size their high-conviction ideas. Patrick is one such reserved and cautious trader. He is covering a universe of 200 stocks, has an elaborate screening process, and is basically trading not to lose. He mentioned that in the past he had done better, but he got off to some early losses and played defense the remainder of the year. He did make money in the second half of the year and ended up $7 million. His risk manager indicated that Patrick had done 3.7 percent returns on gross market value (GMV) while the minimum target on buying power should be 12.5 percent with a Sharpe of 1.5. He noted that Patrick had a low batting average (45 percent) and a low batting average in all time buckets. Despite this, he had a good slugging ratio, making on average more in his winners than he was losing in his losers. He is conventional in his approach and doesn't usually incorporate a broad range of ideas into his decision making.

Patrick is most comfortable when he feels things are under control; so he is inclined to monitor and track the progress of his activities. While he is often timely, he is also reluctant to let go of the details of a trade and may sacrifice efficiency for exactitude. He displays a highly structured, disciplined approach to making investment decisions and will consider the information at his disposal in great detail and systematically evaluate each opportunity. His high standards and cautious tendencies suggest that he will make consistently reliable decisions over time. However, he is not likely to be creative in looking for new opportunities or developing investment strategies. He is formulaic in his approach to risk and reluctant to consider ideas that do not have a proven track record or that do not conform to his preexisting notions. He would be able to act more quickly with fewer names, indicating that he might do well with 15 longs and 15 shorts as opposed to the 20 longs and 20 shorts that he had last year. After much discussion with his risk manager, Patrick finally (reluctantly) committed to a reasonable target of $40 million on $200 million of capital.

Indy is another cautious trader. While he has terrific statistics, a high Sharpe ratio, and excellent drawdown statistics, he is obviously reluctant to get bigger and use his BP. He gets out of all his positions when there are any macro events rather than holding onto his high-conviction ideas. We explored this theme and focused on his inability to deal with loss and the anxiety he experiences when there are small drops of P&L. He is very focused on his daily P&L and was looking for help in finding a way to get bigger.

This pattern was also demonstrated by Toby, who has a well-thought-out process and sound portfolio management construction but is still relatively cautious. This shows up in his good drawdown stats, the absence of illiquidity, and his tendency not to utilize all of his buying power. His statistics in general are average, except that his drawdown management is in the 91st percentile. He had relatively weak performance in his longer-dated trades and only 50 percent of his trades registering as "winners." While he showed a good distribution of conviction, it was clear that he, too, needed to better utilize his buying power limits.

While some traders demonstrate cautiousness in terms of sizing and deploying capital, others show their reserved personalities by trading in illiquid positions. For example, Toby finds it hard to find high-conviction ideas and good shorts. He has not been very successful in finding catalysts. Based on his stats, it appears that his usage of buying power was down, his names were down, and his statistics in general were average. That being said, he had a good percentage of winning trades, but his slugging ratio was low, and there was a tendency toward illiquidity in his portfolio. Toby expressed awareness that he was more active in illiquid names and noted that he was trying to manage his drawdown by selling some. Still, 13 percent of his BP was greater than two days of average daily volume, and he wasn't using all of his BP. Toby obviously needed to find more ideas so he could put bigger positions on the books.

Another example is Jeff, a deep-value PM who has to learn to increase idea velocity and be more focused on P&L results, targeting and getting out of losing positions and getting bigger in high-conviction ideas. He has been struggling to adapt his long-term, deep-value technology investment style to a more goal-oriented hedge fund and has been experiencing some pressure to increase the number of ideas and improve his timing. Shorting has been a problem for him since the value longs don't move with the market, and it has been hard to find shorts. He has relied on IWM indexes but is moving toward using baskets of nonconcentrated shorts. Jeff has begun to look for more short-term catalysts than he has in the past and for names that move.

Up until now, Jeff had 31 completed trades with 20 being in the 21- to 60-day bucket. His percentage of winning trades is 20 percent with a big loss ratio and the possibility that he takes his names off too soon. His book is skewed to the left with losers being bigger than winners. It was suggested that he put more ideas and names into his book. It was noted that once Jeff develops a repeatable and successful process his book will skew to the right. In the 61+ bucket he had 5 trades, three of which worked.

Jeff seems to be a bright guy who is very cautious and tentative but slowly coming around to looking for greater idea velocity, more focus on short-term catalysts, and a greater willingness to redeploy capital into ideas that seem to be working rather than simply buying cheap and holding for the long haul.

The Anxious and Insecure Risk-Taker   Other traders aren't necessarily cautious—they are just fearful or insecure. Morgan, for example, is a very analytical person who weighs the available options, focuses on the details, and considers all the possible consequences. His extreme attention to the "fine print" leads him to be very responsible but also very insecure, relying on conventional approaches rather than innovative methods. Though Morgan prides himself on his ability to manage details, it is a trait that leads to delays in his effort to move tasks and projects forward. He has no sense of urgency, and given his desire for structure, tends to be somewhat of a perfectionist. This can lead to indecision and an inability to function without sufficient information. While Morgan's research abilities would be highly beneficial, he will find it difficult to take risk without some measure of reinforcement. In addition, because he is often slow to act, he may lose out to competitors who are more action oriented.

Another trader, Braxton, is simply afraid of losing. He is afraid of having his capital cut. He is afraid of being fired, and his fear is affecting his performance. Although Braxton is relatively successful and knows how to cut his losers and hold onto his winners, he plays defensively and isn't taking an adequate amount of risk. Despite the fact that he is up about $12.5 million for the year, he rarely uses his capital and has been running between $1.5 million and $2.5 million of his designated $4 million VAR. He has been a successful countertrend trader but admits that he is fearful that if he gets bigger he will lose more and that if he loses too much money he may be fired. He is projecting his own fearfulness onto the firm, even though the boundaries are pretty well-defined, and he has always been guided to make money in a risk-controlled way.

To improve, Braxton needs to make a conscious effort to commit to taking positions that are 10 to 20 percent bigger, since his success up to this time points to the fact that his risk management is good and that if he used more capital and took bigger positions his profitability would increase. He is now feeling more confident about starting to size positions when he has conviction and wants to stop playing defensively.

Some traders demonstrate their insecurity by selling their winners too early, a pattern that typically appears in a holding-period analysis. Here, the winning trade percentage may greatly exceed 50 percent and be quite outsized. However, the average P&L per trade is very small (or negative), and the slugging ratio is very small. The implication is that when the trade becomes a winner, the portfolio manager sells too quickly, thereby not making enough profit to offset losers, which in turn can be outsized.

Some risk-averse PMs are inclined to be more comfortable holding a larger number of positions where no particular position is large (say, less than 2.5 percent of BP). They are not putting enough of their capital at risk in any one position. There is an underlying risk aversion in these traders, many of whom are quite successful in this approach. However, I mention this because it may reflect that the traders are relying on certain personality tendencies rather than a rational strategy based on a full understanding of the risks and stats. These portfolio managers tend to exhibit higher Sharpe ratios, winning trade percentages, and better drawdown control, but they also tend to exhibit lower slugging ratios and tend to put on too many ideas. Therefore, there is a danger that there is not enough capacity for the portfolio manager to differentiate among positions and really obtain an edge in the positions he is trying to follow.

Belton is a good example of someone who needs to do the right kind of work in order to maximize risk. After reviewing his positions last year, Belton discovered that if he excluded his top 10 winners and bottom 10 losers, 70 other trades netted him hardly more than $1 million. He put a lot of effort into a lot of ideas that never amounted to much. His best results were with high-conviction ideas where he had done the work and had the thesis right. This year, he intends to focus on high-conviction ideas where he can put on $8 to $15 million and skip the $1 to $2 million trades. He will run a hedged book but basically be less net long or net short than he was. He believes he can do well with one good idea per month. He is planning to make a few concentrated big bets, hedging them with good shorts. He has no problem finding stocks to short as hedges. He has learned to add to winners and to reduce the size of losers rather than buy losers.

Anxious, insecure, and cautious traders often need to be encouraged to take more risk, something that should be done based on levels of conviction and sized commensurate with the amount of profit that they want to make. This is where I spend a lot of my time encouraging people to *do more work*, to think outside the box, and then to take the risk necessary to make specific amounts of profits.

The Perfectionist Risk-Taker   The perfectionist risk-taker is often smart and knowledgeable and mistaken for being extremely cautious. In reality, his risk-taking style is defined not by a cautious nature but by his perfectionist tendencies. A trader has to be cautious, but *cannot* be a perfectionist. If he waits for perfect information, crossing all the *t*'s and dotting all the *i*'s, he may not be able to make decisions in a timely fashion. This may work for some analysts, but not for portfolio managers.

Take Marc. Marc is a good performer, highly intellectual, and stubborn, which leads him to be too cautious about using all his capital. Marc has excellent statistics with high winning trade percentage, minimal drawdown, good shorts, and high-conviction ideas. But he generally uses only part of his buying power (about 60 percent). Liquidity is not an issue; his liquidity is less than 10 percent of daily volume in most of his positions, and his Sharpe ratio is 3.5. He could certainly take more risk and increase his P&L substantially while maintaining a high Sharpe. His 2 percent drawdown is exemplary, and there is no fear that he will have a significant drawdown if he takes more risk.

But Marc is uncomfortable with his highest-conviction ideas; he starts to question his thesis and begins to find elements that suggest the conviction isn't justified. He actually feels more comfortable with his medium-conviction ideas. He admitted that if his capital were increased he would take more risk, although probably still remain at 60 percent of his buying power, suggesting that perhaps he would use more capital if he had even more buying power. As you can see, his perfectionist streak makes it almost constitutionally impossible for him to go full bore against his buying power.

While successful, he could be extremely more so if he would learn to take a little more risk. He has some of the best statistics in the firm but doesn't use all his capital or put on too many high-conviction ideas. Why? Because he is generally waiting until he gets to 85 percent conviction before he sizes his positions. Since he rarely gets to that level of conviction, he is reluctant to put on his positions in size. To motivate Marc, he has to be reassured that it is okay to use more capital. He needs to be convinced that he will do just fine if he sizes positions where he has 65 or 70 percent conviction, especially given the strength of his trading stats. It was also suggested that he try to get more names in the book and that he begin to size them as well in the effort to take more risk. One year after our discussion, Marc was running more money but still showing the same perfectionist tendencies.

Donovan is another example of a perfectionist risk-taker. He doesn't use his buying power and rarely sizes his ideas in terms of his level of conviction. He has very few high-conviction bets. When challenged about trading to win rather than trading not to lose, he talks about *developing* the process and taking a year to get up to full use of his $100 million of capital. His rationalization for his approach is based on his need to take his time to scale up and his concern for liquidity constraints. His slugging ratio is very low, and it is clear that if he continues to get 60 percent of his trades right and size them correctly and hold them he could increase his profitability. Donovan expressed concern that sizing positions too big might run a risk of a major drawdown if a number of them failed. A probability distribution with binomial expectations showed that the probability of a string of even five losses was negligible, suggesting that Donovan's issue is more of gut-instinct than of mathematical rationality.

* * *

Everyone has a different personality, and personalities are destined to affect how we manage risk. Still, whether stubborn, reserved, anxious, or perfectionist, the best PMs are independent decision makers with an appetite for risk. However, those same characteristics also make for a tendency to break the rules and take bigger chances than risk management believes is wise. So, even if a trader has an excellent personal history and a personality fit for risk-taking greatness, it is still necessary to make sure that risk-takers adhere to the risk guidelines of the firm and don't become total buccaneers.

LEARNING TO UPGRADE YOUR PERFORMANCE

Unfortunately, not all traders recognize the importance of risk management. As obvious as it would seem to be, many traders simply dismiss or undervalue how vital it is to success. Alex is one such trader, and his inability to manage risk is evident in his current frustration. He believes he could be bigger but has reached his limit on sizing (15 percent of his portfolio). He is also net long about 35 percent (also at his limit). He believes his volatility at 6 percent is not that high and that he is "right" even though he is in a huge drawdown. He believes that long term his ideas will be right and cannot understand why the firm won't hedge out his risk. I confronted him about this and strongly advised him to follow good risk management principles and try to keep his losses down to stay in the game. While he was very appreciative of the attention and support and appreciates the importance of risk management, he is still of the mind that the risk manager cannot understand what it feels like to trade ideas when you have done the work. I talked to him about establishing a template for assessing shorts from a stock-selection and risk-management viewpoint—combining fundamentals and technicals, looking for companies with bad accounting, low multiples (with high expectations), and smaller caps. In all this, he needs to learn to raise his threshold of awareness of what constitutes a good short and how to manage risk better. I indicated that it was up to each PM to control his own risk and suggested that he get some better idea of how to assess his volatility.

It is very important that PMs learn early on to stay within their limits. Limits are in place for the benefit of the portfolio manager as well as for the firm. In the event that a particular opportunity presents itself to any portfolio manager that would put the manager outside of some preagreed limit, the portfolio manager should discuss the opportunity with risk management. Decisions about whether to exceed any limit are at the discretion of risk management. This was the essence of a conversation I had during a PM review with Samuel.

Samuel had a problem staying within the defined limits. This became especially significant in periods of major drawdowns in the markets when not only did he put himself at risk but his firm as well. This pattern emerged in 2006, and was again apparent in midyear reviews in 2007. Essentially, it appeared that Samuel didn't think the rules applied to him; therefore it was necessary to confront him about this until he acknowledged that he would play by the rules. Samuel needed to learn how to recognize drawdown triggers and to start conversations with risk management about delevering his portfolio in an effort to catch his losses early enough in the process to prevent a serious drawdown.

The big thing in managing a portfolio is to keep the NMV within reasonable limits—meaning that the book is hedged to take out the market risk. So when the gross market value or the capital is increased, sometimes the net is reduced, which means that the portfolio has to be run with a hedge on, so many shorts to balance out the long and not more than 20 or 25 percent of the portfolio in shorts. So, someone running a hedged book might have $176 million in longs and $94 million in shorts, giving them $82 million or the difference between the longs and shorts as their NMV, meaning that they have only $82 million in exposed long positions. This is the way a PM can deploy more capital and yet do it in a risk-managed way.

Of course, not everyone is willing to run his book in terms of these risk constraints, so eventually the risk manager will not apportion more capital to the trader if he goes over the net limits. This sometimes works as a way of keeping traders in line. Sometimes it doesn't work, especially when people have difficulty hearing criticism and adhering to rules.

Too many traders don't understand risk-taking in a managed way. It is important to take risk in a big way but only when you have built up a reserve of capital. I like to point out how important it is to follow risk management principles, certain statistical metrics to make sure that the trader is doing what he ought to be doing and maximizing his trading strengths.

Consider Chuck. Chuck has been having a hard time. He is down about $3 million for the year, and his buying power has been reduced from $50 million to $35 million. For the past six years before coming to the firm, he focused mainly on directional bets, playing momentum and flow. This strategy no longer seems to be working, and he is trying to find a new approach that is profitable. He has lowered his yearly target from $10 million to $5 million, which means he needs to make $50,000 per day to overcome his present loss and reach the target of $5 million. He is well aware that his performance as a PM has been substandard, but attributes it to difficulties of the market.

We talked about running a more concentrated portfolio built around companies that he knows, sizing down his positions relative to his capital levels, reducing his conviction sizing, and diversifying his portfolio so that he can work his way back up. I suggested that he needs to be more proactive in reviewing his portfolio daily to find imminent opportunities and to see what he missed and what he needs to incorporate into his process to increase his hit ratio.

As we discussed in the last chapter, you have to develop a goal and a strategy for reaching that goal. Part of that strategy involves laying out in a detailed way how you plan on handling risk. Even traders who are doing well can find an area in which to improve.

Adam is up about $4.7 million for the year. He is definitely feeling more confident about his performance and continues to focus on getting bigger in high-conviction ideas where he has done the work, to pare down when the ideas aren't working, and to keep getting out of stale shorts and not let them bleed too much. He manages his capital by managing each position and the overall portfolio.

To the extent that his stocks move in tandem and in response to macro events, he tries to manage his overall exposure in terms of basic material risk. He knows the supply/demand curve in most of his metals and is able to integrate this knowledge into his trading approach. But he doesn't believe that he can find any more macro inputs that would help him anticipate the moves in the market, although his biggest drawdowns have been secondary to macro moves.

While Adam has become more nimble and thinks that he is sensitive to these issues and can handle them, the problem is that the macro lead indicators keep changing with different implications, so that it is hard to prepare in advance for them. In discussing illiquid stocks, he noted that the best-valued stocks are generally illiquid and at the lower end of market-cap scale. The best opportunities are in the lower-cap names. He also noted that he prefers this game since he doesn't think he is good at the momentum game, which drives the more liquid, larger-cap stocks. So, he has a very good conviction and idea flow but needs some tweaking on closing out positions on ideas submitted. He has agreed to work on the template and high-conviction criteria, and to provide portfolio updates in order to improve these areas of risk management.

Another critical issue here is generating enough original ideas to populate the portfolio with high-conviction ideas that are going to move far and produce certain probabilistic results by way of achieving a stated goal or target. By reverse-engineering a trading strategy, based on the expected results, and calculating winning percentage and W/L ratio, the portfolio manager ought to be able to determine how many ideas he needs to generate and what kinds of returns he can expect in each of his positions. This goal-oriented approach acts as the driver of the research process and the quality and velocity of ideas that must be generated. Paul, who manages a large team of analysts and portfolio managers, explained to me recently how he has created a system to help him manage risk in this way:

> *You have to start your hedging on an idea-by-idea basis. We have a system where I have grouped every bet on the short or long side of a book to balance risk. I look at the net exposure of that group. I know when I roll that all up I can look at the net exposure of the portfolio. By looking at it on a position-by-position basis, then rolling it all out, you actually get a more true risk management between your longs and your shorts. How do you come up with a hedge on it? Recognize that one answer might be, there is none, and this has to be your directional exposure. How do we think about a hedge and then fill a position? Break it down qualitative and quantitative. On the qualitative side, the question that I ask is, "What is it about the bet that I am making that's outside of management's control?" The quantitative way is to basically do a search for companies that have a high statistical correlation to the position that you have. Then you can go through and say, "Which of these fit into the qualitative issues, the qualitative factors that were identified?" When you can actually come up with the best cases, a basket of ten to twenty names that are exposed to the same factors, update them on a day-to-day basis and*

see if they move in the same direction. The last component is, how volatile is that basket relative to your name? Correlation of positions shows your direction. Volatility is going to show you magnitude.

It's going to be easy to find longs; so at least this gives you an option to responsibly manage risk. Instead of having ten longs and ten shorts, you are actually increasing your idea velocity at some level by not having to find a lot of marginal stuff to populate a portfolio. You are getting more concentrated, but you are not doing it in an irresponsible way. You are not going to have big drawdowns for market-related reasons. It's a way of gaming a system and making it easier.

Of course, sizing, like most aspects of trading, can also be a very emotional one. Traders tend to fall in love with ideas and size them according to their level of affection. Unfortunately, this often leads to an unhealthy attachment so that when events happen and the position turns against them, they fail to get out. In fact, they often wind up adding to losing positions and in a deeper hole. In addition, when they do get out they are so emotionally spent that they are unable to get back in the game in a timely manner.

Paul tries to keep himself at a safe distance from such emotional attachment:

I am going to cut the position that I love because I just lost too much money. I have enough confidence in my ability to make money over time that I don't want to be emotionally attached to one situation and have that be my focus, be my whole life. We are trying to predict the future. As long as you have cash, you can play. You can earn back whatever you lost and make a rate of return. Once you get to dollar zero, its game-over for you. Some people have unlimited risk tolerance and don't care how much they go down. They only respond to cutting positions when the risk manager taps them on the shoulder. That's not a good way to approach trading. A better approach is to cut positions when things aren't working, just for the sake of moving and getting into an offensive mindset. The whole point of it is to get freed up into positive situations and not spend time on these negative situations that are going to draw in emotional energy.

Like Paul, the master trader will not invest himself in any of his ideas. He will not allow himself to believe that his decisions define his personality.

While he is concerned with the results, he doesn't allow that concern to lead to bad decisions. He will not size a position solely based on how he feels about it, and he won't stay in a losing position just to prove a point.

So, when sizing positions, first consider how much money you will make if your position turns out to be right. For example, if one position will, at best, make 30 percent and another will make only 5 percent, why would you size them the same dollar amount? Size them appropriately relative to the percentage you expect to earn from them. Then, when a trade is not going your way, take the time to consider what you did wrong. Think about how you reacted to the circumstances. To be proactive, prepare yourself for a variety of scenarios by actually visualizing different events and how you will react to each one.

Of course, experience plays a large part in risk management decisions as well. As you develop more experience, you will have a wider spectrum from which to draw ideas and other resources as well as a better handle on how to navigate the difficult trading waters.

Again, referencing trading statistics is also useful in underscoring the kinds of things that are working and aren't working and to begin to suggest what you must focus on to produce improved results. It is important to note that the risk manager's view is that you need at least six months of trading stats to begin to develop a trading profile so as to be able to have an intelligent discussion with a PM. Whereas these statistics point to trends and patterns that you should be conscious of, in the vast majority of instances you cannot simply modify your trading so as to produce better stats. You need to understand what you are doing and try to take these things into consideration as you begin to manage a portfolio.

Understanding the statistics in and of themselves is not sufficient to be able to provide a blueprint for success. It is no different than baseball stats. If the batter strikes out a lot, it is important to point that out to him, but you don't go from the strikeout statistic to batting technique. You find ways of improving your performance by gathering data, evaluating the path to getting paid, and paying attention to drawdown propensity or your personal tendency toward illiquidity and to your holding periods so that you can begin to do the kinds of things that will increase your chances of success.

Portfolio management must be wedded to a research process. You have to find original ideas in a strategically based approach to what has been called the *variant perception*—nonconsensus ways of seeing the world and the markets that provide for a differentiated and positive view of stocks. This requires an additional skill set of seeing around corners, dealing with the unknown, and being able to work with insufficient information and perspective by creating an original way of looking at the world. We will explore this strategic, original way of thinking in the next several chapters.

 CHAPTER IN REVIEW

1. Successful risk-taking behavior is the ability to take risk in a controlled way, follow the rules, manage drawdowns, cull losers, add to winners, express conviction in ideas in terms of sizing, and use capital appropriately.

2. The successful trader is a goal-oriented risk-taker with good abstract reasoning and not too much cautiousness or thoroughness that might interfere with his ability to trade stocks in his portfolio. He is able to run balanced books, get bigger when he has an edge, and take risks in calculated ways.

3. You can learn to assess risk-taking ability by considering a person's trading philosophy, how he handles drawdowns, and the certain mix of passion and dedication within himself.

4. In order to become a winning trader, a PM must be willing to review risk statistics with the risk manager so as to find ways of improving his overall performance, to examine personality factors that are likely to influence his risk management skills, and to explore various strategies that can upgrade his performance.

5. By looking at a trader's profitability or P&L, his percent of winning trades, his slugging ratio or W/L ratio, as well as his Sharpe ratio and other risk statistics from his previous job, it is possible to identify certain behavioral patterns that are reflective of his overall past performance. A lot of these factors are secondary to underlying psychological patterns, and from them you can make certain assumptions about future performance.

6. Personality can also play a significant part in how a trader takes risk. If an individual is too cautious or too thorough or in a psychological sense too much of a perfectionist, he is likely to have difficulty in adapting to a goal-oriented, high-performance approach to portfolio management. In addition, it is important to screen out traders who are too impulsive, impatient, and perhaps irrational risk-takers who lack sufficient cautiousness and thoroughness to prevent them from blowing up.

7. Even if a trader has an excellent personal history and a personality fit for risk-taking greatness, it is still necessary to make sure that risk-takers

adhere to the risk guidelines of the firm and don't become total buccaneers. Therefore, it is very important that PMs learn early on to stay within their limits. It is important to take risk in a big way, but only when you have built up a reserve of capital.

8. As discussed in the previous chapter, you have to develop a goal and a strategy for reaching that goal. Part of that strategy involves laying out in a detailed way how you plan on handling risk. Even traders who are doing well can find an area in which to improve.

CHAPTER 4

Thinking Outside the Box

The Importance of Ingenuity

Original creative ideas are innovative because no one has ever thought about them before. Those who develop such ideas are usually thinking in a different way than others. Consider Copernicus and how he said that the earth traveled around the sun, or Einstein when he introduced the Theory of Relativity. When these concepts were introduced, they were new and controversial. It took a while for everyone else to catch on.

Academic studies have shown that fundamental datapoints (earnings, corporate actions, etc.) explain roughly 30 percent of daily/weekly stock price variation. Given that fundamentals are only one of many factors that determine stock price, it is crucial to understand what other factors play a role in determining stock prices.

In order to make money in the markets, a trader needs to know something that other people don't know yet. He needs to be thinking ahead of the curve, to anticipate what is going to happen before there is evidence in the markets that it is going to happen and everyone starts to get on board with the same trading hypothesis. To do that, he has to understand something about the company and how it is functioning, how the particular industry is doing, what is going on in the economy, and a variety of other things. The more he knows, the more he can make a calculation about the likely target or trajectory the stock is going to follow. The more work he does, the more he is ahead of others and the earlier he gets into his position. This leads to more confidence in the position and a greater chance of success.

CASE STUDY ON THE SATISFACTION OF CREATIVE THINKING

In this conversation, an experienced hedge fund manager named Peter explains the emotional and financial satisfaction that comes with thinking creatively.

Kiev: Can you talk about variant perception and the discomfort of having an idea before it's right? Does just knowing that it's a variant perception kind of excite you in an uncomfortable way?

Peter: If you could make forty percent in two names, one with the crowd and the other against the crowd, from a dollar perspective you should be totally indifferent. From an emotional perspective you should choose to make it with the crowd. It's just easier. You don't even have to think about it. But there is no question that I would rather make the other forty percent. Psychologically, I get a "Jones" out of being the only kid in the room to have figured out the problem. Everybody else is wrong, and I am right. I realize the dollars are the same. I realize the efficiency is easier on the other one.

K: That's the satisfaction you get from being ahead of the crowd. How about the *need* to be ahead of the crowd to make more money? Is that a fallacy?

P: Do you need to do it in order to make money? I think I do.

K: Do you think everyone does?

P: I just don't know. I look at the great investors who have made a lot of money, and I think more often than not they are contrary.

K: What about being uncomfortable with knowing something that others don't know? Are you willing to take that pain, getting in early on before there is any kind of visibility?

P: Yeah; I don't mind sitting in a room and listening to everybody else be wrong, just kind of quietly smiling, and as the stock goes down I will just buy more. I am in the business to make money and deliver performance. I get psychic income out of being right.

Short-sellers probably get even more psychic income about being one in a crowd. They don't get any economic income for the times they're not right.

K: Do you put any value on somebody presenting an idea that is original? Do you encourage them to be comfortable with being uncomfortable because they know something that seems impossible?

P: We haven't said it that way. We haven't encouraged people to more aggressively research scenarios where if they get conviction they are just so off-consensus that the opportunity is great but they may be awkward walking into a business. So, we haven't actively encouraged that. We do it from the negative. "Don't bring the ordinary ideas." We haven't said, but maybe we should, "Go out and try to find extraordinary ideas other than through the return on capital."

K: Are you finding there is a need to discover new ways of looking at stocks? Are you looking for new angles on the game because the game has gotten more crowded?

P: I think we are still trying to accomplish exactly what we used to try to accomplish. We just have more capabilities and a few more tools at our disposal in order to accomplish those things more effectively and more efficiently to a greater extent. We don't see it as the game has changed. We see it as our resources have grown.

The best traders, like Peter, have a strategic edge and are able to adapt their approach based on new information and not become fixed in a position because of previous analyses. To the extent that the trader has good abstract reasoning ability and is conceptually oriented he should be able to adapt to a variety of situations and come up with original solutions.

THE STRATEGIC THINKER

Many people imagine that they are creative thinkers, when in fact they are implementers, maximizers, goal-oriented pragmatists, but not necessarily skilled at dealing with the unknown or planning the future based on experience in functioning in uncharted territories.

Ideally, the strategic trader is someone who can *think outside the box*. Whether he is a candidate for a PM role with a good academic record or someone who has worked his way up as an apprentice, the strategic trader is someone who understands the complexities of financial models, business drivers, a sector or industry, as well as company-specific metrics and who can make probabilistic bets on how companies are going to do so that he can blend his understanding of the company's performance with prognostic statements about what is possible. The strategic thinker has the ability to function with limited information and to deal with the unforeseen events without guarantees or certainty.

This kind of trader will be comfortable dealing with unprovable events or the tails of events rather than having to rely on consensus or conventional ways of approaching problems. This edge gives the trader an ability to see the world in a unique way, to see patterns where others simply see complexity. Aware of these patterns, he thinks strategically, always playing out alternative scenarios, always asking: "What if *this* happened, then what?" He is always considering different options. He first considers what makes stocks high-probability investments and focuses on elements of the setup of the trade that can compel the trade.

By continually asking these kinds of *what-if* questions, the strategic trader is able to see around the next corner so as to be able to evaluate potential obstacles. Guided by the different paths before him, he is able to start making selections, discarding the paths that lead nowhere or the ones that lead to resistance. When he sees clarity, he is able to take decisive action.

Over time, strategic thinkers develop a high tolerance for ambiguity and uncertainty, or what psychologists call *cognitive dissonance*, and to engage in the necessary work to support this view. In effect, they have learned to be comfortable living in the gap between what is known and what is yet to be realized, which is the essence of thinking in a nonconsensus way.

CASE STUDY ON LEARNING TO BE CREATIVE

I had the good fortune of talking to Jesse, who teaches a specific investment research process to his analysts when they first start working with him. His approach underscores some of the ways that the best investment minds transmit knowledge of their approach to the next generation of investors.

This discussion is worth including by way of showing how someone can be taught to think creatively. In addition, it supports my view that, with some effort, traders can develop a variant perception and unearth data that the rest of the Street hasn't yet discovered.

Kiev: What's your view of the variant perception as a critical factor for creative thinking, and does it increase the probability that the bet is going to pay off?

Jesse: I teach the importance of what I call the *tension point*. The challenge is to find the tension point in the investment. Because of the complexity of a company, you want to figure out where that tension is and what's behind it. Each company is going to have two or three things that really matter. I interchangeably use them. They are key factors and tension points. The best investments are where Wall Street doesn't even know the tension points. A tension point is the key factor that's going to drive the path of the investment, not the company. They might be one and the same. What's going to determine the path of the investment?

K: To get to where the value is unlocked?

J: If the stock is twenty dollars today, what's going to determine whether it's a forty-dollar stock or a ten-dollar stock over a certain period of time?

K: You think it's a forty-dollar stock because you know certain things about it, but it's not yet forty dollars. Certain things have to happen to get it to forty.

J: That's how it works in the real world. With my analysts, I assign each of them to a company. They are not going to have a thesis going in. So, what they're going to do is look through with a fresh slate to figure out what are the factors that are going to determine whether this is a long or a short. They are going to look for the tension points that are going to be driving it. I assign them stocks that are pretty binary. There are two pieces to the framework. One is figuring out what matters most. That's the tension point, and that could be whether a new product is going to have fast adoption. It could be whether housing prices are going to fall significantly. It could be that Croc Shoe has peaked in popularity, and it was just a fad, and now it's going to fall significantly. So that's coming up with a tension point.

So, they start from scratch. They have to go in and figure out what's the real tension point. Then they have to do research so that they understand which path or how that tension point is going to unfold better than any noninsider; that's the framing. As part of that, they are looking for catalysts like on a signpost instead of looking for little things on the margin.

They then compare it. They figure out what the company's fundamentals are going to do. Then they compare it to consensus. Most of them develop a very significant variant perception. They are going to spend twelve weeks on one company. The hope is that by the time they finish this assignment they know what matters most and how it's going to unfold better than Wall Street.

K: What is it that enables the guy to get a nonconsensus view, to know that what he knows is something that other people don't know because he has gone where no one else has gone? Is he comfortable dealing with new sources of information or new ways of looking at a company and doing original research that is off the beaten track or outside the box as opposed to Wall Street consensus kind of fundamental analysis?

J: Because these guys are so fresh, we come out of it backwards. Here is what we said; "You can't talk to management, sell-side, any company executives and the Street. You have to do very creative, primary research without knowing any of that, and then come to your own conclusions."

K: So, they can't do the conventional stuff, and they're forced to think originally.

J: The research that is done in this process is mindboggling. They can't do anything that a normal analyst would do.

K: Are they given any guidance about how to do original creative work?

J: Oh, yeah! We talk about this all the time. Without doing any of the conventional stuff, you can be in shock and awe at how you think the Street is just missing at the very end.

K: Do they have any background in fundamental research?

J: Well, they generally have some banking experience or have already worked as a junior analyst at another shop.

K: Who are the best guys?

J: The best guys are people who "get it"; it's just intuitive to them. They are willing to go out there and just do the work. They summarize really clearly.

K: What are some examples of creative research?

J: Last year, one of my analysts was looking at a certain bank, and he was doing analysis with management to see what he was dealing with. It was not a subprime lender, but close enough. He went and found some public database. He could search and figure out what were the homes this guy owned, whether he had been divorced, just to get some character on this CEO.

There was a company that one guy was looking at, and he actually went out and talked to people. He said, "If I were interested in building an XYZ plant, how much would it cost me? How long would it take to build it?"

People visit stores. They go on the Better Business Bureau. They will get all of the complaints of the UK Better Business Bureau. One analyst went to Weight Watchers and went through the program and talked to counselors. They do a lot of interesting numbers stuff in terms of just slicing and dicing the numbers.

Conventional stuff, practically speaking, lets you shortcut a lot. The best people find the mix. They leverage the conventional stuff where it can be leveraged. They find the places where the nonconventional is key to adding the value. They find that balance. These analysts are going to have one idea for twelve weeks—nothing else. They will spend a third of their time on this project, if not more. However, in the real world, you are going to have ten, fifteen, or twenty companies.

K: What's their view of the value of the experience longer term?

J: I think the most powerful takeaway is that people learn up-front that if they just stick to the nonconventional they can know the company. They have an inner conviction that they know what's going to unfold, what's important, better than the experts.

The reality is that ninety percent of the analysts don't apply it after they finish the project. The lesson stays with them; they know they should.

K: It's unconventional. That's what I am getting at; it takes a tremendous amount of psychological courage to deal with the original way of looking at things.

J: I agree. That's a big part of it, and then another big part of it is that a lot of the Wall Street organizations are already so entrenched. You need even more courage to go in as a new employee and do this type of thing. That takes a lot of courage and isn't acceptable in a lot of places.

While there may be a shortage of traders who use these creative research techniques, there is no denying that a good PM develops a strategic approach to idea generation based on a comprehensive research process.

He reduces his overall exposure to the markets during drawdown periods by getting out of marginal ideas where he lacks a true edge, and develops a view that differs from consensus, with a well-defined set of upcoming catalysts or events such as earnings announcements and product launches that are likely to increase the probability-weighted chance that his bet will pay off. He has hedging strategies to take out the market risk and reduces the overall amount of risk he is taking by way of lining himself up for a successful and profitable recovery when the downturn ceases. Moreover, he takes pride in his ability to function quite independently of the herd. When a trader has this kind of high degree of abstract reasoning ability and the ability to think creatively, he is more likely to generate original investment ideas at a sufficient velocity to keep pace with allocated capital and stretch targets.

At a subsequent interview with Jesse, I had a more in-depth discussion about this kind of strategic thinking that is worth recounting since it describes a bit of the psychological process associated with dealing with the nonconsensus investment process.

Jesse: What I love is looking for situations where there is a real extreme. People are hardwired to think something has happened, something that is at an extreme, and the world believes it will never change; yet there is evidence that it is changing. Because it's gone on for so long and so far, the world doesn't see it.

Kiev: What's an example of something that is at an extreme?

J: I look for a story based on an absolute belief, for instance, that Japanese banks are the worst in the world and they will never be profitable again.

K: So you're looking for the absolute belief in something. Then you look for the data that disprove that belief?

J: Yes.

K: You're really looking at superstitions that aren't true.

J: I never thought that would be who I am, but that's it. That's when the hair stands on my neck, when I see it unraveling. That's when I get that chemical feeling.

K: How unique is this way of thinking about the markets?

J: I feel like it's very unique. I wouldn't trade it for anything. I find very few people who think like I do. I think part of how valuable we will be in the future will depend on thinking this way. Take energy. I said, "Hey, for ten years energy has been an unprofitable enterprise. That can't last." Now, we have some evidence that demand is growing, and that supply is shrinking. This is one of the things that I am working on.

K: What's all this depending on?

J: Evidence of change. I've been known to take very large positions with incredibly high conviction. With these situations, typically there is very low downside risk and there is evidence of change. If you can't lose much, then you can make a ton. That's what attracts me to it.

K: Is that what Warren Buffett does?

J: No; he is totally different. These companies aren't great companies.

K: They're at a low value.

J: When I believe that the whole world is wrong in terms of their beliefs, I feel really comfortable.

K: You start getting uncomfortable when the world starts believing what you believe at the beginning of the up cycle?

J: I get less comfortable as the price of oil advances, even though I can visualize where it could go better than most.

K: You don't see the increased momentum as an opportunity?

J: I am working on it. It's one of my written goals, trying to understand it when I'm feeling uncomfortable.

K: You probably still need to find out who out there still believes oils are a short. There may be less superstition, but there is still superstition.

J: I think that's a great point.

K: You still can have a contrarian view. Your unique way of seeing opportunities and seeing the value in existing beliefs or superstitions seems to be a strategic gift that you have.

J: It's fascinating; literally, I get so comfortable in knowing something that no one else can see or accept.

K: Most people are consensus thinkers. They are not going to get in at the bottom of the curve or at the inflection point at the top before something starts going down.

J: I think that's it, because they are playing for things that appear to be more fully developed and more certain, after some of the initial value has been taken out of the bet. They are not comfortable early on before the longer-term trading theme is starting to emerge. I can sit all day looking for situations like this. When it starts to take off or to unravel, I can feel the energy. When it's actually unraveling, I feel a tremendous burst of energy.

This interview illustrates how investors have to learn how to deal with difficult-to-predict events as opportunities for developing the variant perception and developing an edge in their investment process. Of particular interest is what Jesse says about the excitement he experiences when he discovers a nonconsensus superstition or widely held immutable belief, which he believes is the first stage in developing an investment theme. Much of this has to do with his capacity to function with a great deal of uncertainty created by discovering a nonconsensus idea.

IDEA CONSTRUCTION

As Jesse's interview illustrates, thinking creatively involves much more than buying good companies and shorting bad ones. Sometimes, the most innovative trades involve the most unexpected moves. The key is to look for inefficiency in the market and to focus more on issues of psychology, game theory, and behavioral finance than on fundamentals.

In order to truly be successful, you must recognize factors in the market that might have an impact on the price of the stock during a specific time period. Ideally, you should develop a differentiated view and decipher the data to determine which trades have the most potential before investing a large percentage of time investigating them.

DEVELOPING A VARIANT PERCEPTION

Variant perception was first introduced by Michael Steinhardt about 20 years ago to underscore the fact that the best way to make money in the markets is to know something that others don't yet know, to think ahead of the curve, and to anticipate when something is going to happen.

To do that, you have to understand something about the company and how it is functioning, how the particular industry is doing, what is going on in the economy, and a variety of other things. The more you know, the more you can make a calculation about the likely target or trajectory the stock is going to follow because you have done the work.

One critical part of the work in developing a variant view is to focus on stories with an element of change. The presence of change is important because where there is change, there is the potential for different outcomes, which equals investment opportunity. Change can take the form of new management, new products, and new market opportunities. Review a whole checklist of items before earnings to increase your sense of the probability of being paid in terms of short-term, quarterly, and annual earnings, options, management, what the sell-side is saying, and what makes stocks high-probability investments. Ask yourself the following questions:

- Is there an element of change and a clear path to getting paid?
- How much does the thesis depend on internal or external factors?
- What are the catalysts; what are you playing for?
- Have you quantified the results?
- How does your outlook differ from that of others?
- How much of the thesis is internally driven by the company?
- What is your conviction level?
- What is the upside/downside probability of getting fundamentals right?
- What is the probability of getting paid if you are right?
- Has any sort of expectational analysis been done to gauge what is "in the stock"?
- Is this really an absolute-return call, or is this a relative-performance call?
- Should this idea be hedged?
- Are there macro/sector risks that the analyst didn't consider?
- Could you actually lose even if your thesis is right?

CASE STUDY ON CREATIVE THINKING

This dialogue gives examples of how to find original, creative ways of looking at companies in a nonconsensus way. This is critical by way of demonstrating how a PM must think independently. There is inherent discomfort when thinking in terms of variant perception. So, how can you be empowered and ready to step up to the challenge, and how can you empower your team to do so as well, especially during crisis periods?

Kiev: How do you deal with the fact that with Reg FD it is particularly difficult to get an edge on companies? How do you develop a nonconsensus or variant perception with the limited amount of information available?

Tom: Five years ago, before Reg FD, everyone would get involved in cleanup trades, buying the last two million shares that a large mutual fund was selling. Today, the large mutual funds are V whopping all their trades, trading them at an evaluated average price. Today the blowout decisions are being made by hedge funds. One of their dynamics is that mutual funds don't like to have losers on their sheets when they have to report what stocks they hold to their investors. It's not an economic decision; it's a psychological decision. They don't earn a dollar more if they're less invested in these stocks. I mean, if they had losers and they don't show up on the sheet when they publish their quarterly reports, they still had losers. They just don't want to answer the questions about them. So, opportunities arise when people sell or buy stocks for noneconomic reasons such as wanting to impress investors.

We always make money when people go from fundamental to emotional decision making. We try as hard as we can to be the fundamental people and not be the emotional people. It's hard to maintain objectivity. That may cause me to have a slightly bigger drawdown than the guy who is emotional, but my draw-up is going to be bigger.

Now we are trading as hedge funds. When the opportunity gets kind of big, it may get very big because everybody then is trying to sell it, but that means there are some losses. We may need to leave something in reserve during the time that everything is good and not use all of our gross exposure, and not use all our risk. Then we have a lot more dry powder when everybody else panics.

We are doing all that we can right now to not panic while everybody else is panicking. What we are not doing is taking advantage of this. If everybody is having a five percent drawdown and then the market normalizes, if we had more dry powder coming into it, we would have three-and-a-half percent drawdown and a ten percent up-move. Instead, we are going to go down five and up five, like everybody else.

K: So you overextend it?

T: We were overexposed from a gross-exposure basis, from which, after two-and-a-half years of "It's working," one gets kind of lulled into sleep. Every time we have had dry powder, all it has done is cost us a point a month. We could have been using it in our portfolio and making even more money. I think psychologically we all tend to over-wait the trend a little bit too much. We all tend to extrapolate a little bit too much.

So, the lesson is to do pattern recognition as to which one is real and which one is not. When you see all of a sudden things fundamentally change, you can't derisk fast enough! The only way to derisk is just to take stuff that you have on the sheets longer or shorter, whatever, and just reduce it.

If the stocks open all down ten, it wouldn't be rational to derisk because if we did this every time we saw it, we would flinch a lot of times that we shouldn't have. So, to a certain extent there's a balance in reducing risk when you move from "we know" to "we don't know." What's the price of that? How do you measure that? That's where liquidity and crowdedness come into that decision. It's that single decision, when we come in the next day or wake up the next morning and Katrina is pounding the shores of the United States, and refineries are getting knocked out and gas prices are going up. How is that going to affect our stocks? I don't know. If you don't know, you should get out.

As the marketplace becomes more and more efficient, it is important to develop investment theses that differentiate you from other investors. The variant view is based on a *bottom-up* methodology rather than a *top-down* one, each thesis having a particular story that creates a variant view on valuation and with specific future catalysts to close the gap and drive relative appreciation.

The key is to determine whether the market is inefficiently pricing the odds and, if it is doing so, to be confident about making the bet. This means looking for nuances in sentiment and potential for stock appreciation that occur in shorter time horizons, from six months to two years, rather than in longer time horizons, where you might be looking for value creation and value destruction.

You have to be able to understand supply and demand as the drivers of stock prices and recognize always what is going to create incremental buyers—what events will lead more people to buy the stock because of increased demand for a limited amount of stock. If you are shorting a stock, you have to be able to articulate what's going to create incremental *sellers*. This approach seeks to find an edge by increasing the velocity of ideas that are being developed and in particular focusing on what it will take to increase the probability of being paid if you are right in a limited time horizon.

Idea Evaluation Checklist

One trader provided the following Idea Evaluation Checklist, which can help traders conduct an expanded study of companies. It is not a definitive list, but I have included it by way of illustrating the kinds of data needed to support a variant view.

IDEA EVALUATION CHECKLIST

The Elevator Pitch:

❑ Does the thesis incorporate an element of change?
❑ Is there a clear path to getting paid?
❑ Is there quantifiable upside and downside along the path?
❑ How much of the thesis is external versus internal?

Questions to Think Through:

1. Turbo-triggers:

    a. What specific variables have the most impact on stock price?

    b. What is my forecast, and how does it differ from consensus and management guidance? What is driving the difference?

    c. Post release, where will consensus estimates and management guidance move?

    d. What is the time horizon before things move? Why?

2. Sell-side:

    a. Recent changes in ratings?

    b. Estimate revision history: Bar too high or low? Implied growth? Whisper number?

    c. Dispersion of estimates: Does it look like analysts have no clue because of wide dispersion? More risk = more opportunity.

    d. Surprise history: Do they always beat consensus? What happened during the last several Qs, and what happened to the stock?

    e. Comps: Is this an industry where comps matter? Do comps look "easy" or "hard"?

3. Valuation:

    a. Recent price and technicals: Are people selling the stock to avoid event risk? Does everyone hate/love the name?

    b. Relative performance: How have they done versus sector, market?

    c. Valuation: Absolute, relative to industry, and relative to market. Time series: Is this the absolute cheapest it's been? Are there bands?

4. Management approach:

    a. Quality of earnings: Do they beat because of charges, acquisitions, accruals? EPS versus CF divergence?

    b. Guidance style: Always conservative or aggressive? Is there a new team planning a bath?

    c. Guidance history: Do they give it? Do they boost? Is the year back-end loaded or linear?

5. Sentiment:

    a. How did the stock perform over the past two weeks versus market and peer group (outperformance = high expectations)?

    b. SI: Changes, historical trends.

    c. Accounting or short-sell reports: How many? When did they come out? Who did it? What was the impact?

    d. Recent articles: Tone? *BusinessWeek/Barrons* curse?

    e. Presentations: How have they altered perception?

6. Insiders:

    a. Recent activity: Buying matters. Selling hard to gauge.

    b. Company buyback: Magnitude of buyback?

    c. Holdings analysis: Who is in a position hedge funds versus mutual funds?

7. Volatility:

    a. Options: Implied vols? Put volume?

    b. General vol: Panic or excitement?

8. Macro:

    a. Industry feel: Are laterals beating and going down? Blowups?

    b. Economic trends: Homebuilders? Oil? War? Yield curve?

9. Calls to make:

    a. Recent trading flow

    b. Sales coverage

    c. Analysts

    d. Buy-side

    e. Company and management (different read than the Street?)

10. Quantifying conviction:

  a. Quality of expectational gap?

  b. Quality of event path?

  c. Quality of catalysts along the event path?

  d. Quality of the valuation work and price targets?

  e. Quantify up and downside (if my estimates are right, if Street is right, etc). What are the probabilities?

  f. How long will it take and what is the annualized return?

DEFINING EXPECTATIONAL ANALYSIS

The expectational gap is another way of expressing Steinhardt's concept of variant perception. The objective is to do research that supports a variant perception in terms of where a stock is and where you expect it will be when its full value is realized. In expectational analysis, you are asking what factors will take place in order for a specific stock to go from its current value to what you consider its full value.

The magnitude of the *expectational gap* is directly proportional to the amount that you actually expect to get paid. The larger the gap between where the price is and where you expect it to be, once value is unlocked, the more profit you can make. The clearer and shorter the event path, the more likely you are to get paid if you are right. The better you can articulate that gap and the more research and tools you can apply to determine the path to getting paid, the more you can expect to make. The key is to be able to determine why the stock is inefficiently priced.

For example, let's say that the Street values a stock at 20, but from your original work, you know that the stock has more value built into it that the Street hasn't yet realized. You think that the stock could reach its full value at 50. That is your variant perception, what you know about the stock that is not yet known by the Street, based on your research, your talks with the company, your understanding of how a catalyst will go, and so forth. So, the critical questions to ask yourself are:

- What do you know that will increase your chances of getting paid when you bet on this particular stock?

- How do you maximize your chances of getting paid if you get the analysis right and see something that is implicit in the present stock price that has not as yet been expressed?
- What is in the stock?
- What are the implied odds?

Of course, you want to be able to articulate what it is about the trade that makes it interesting to pursue. Some analysts may actually spend two days reading the K, reading the Q, finding out all about the company, where it's located, and the names of every person on the management team, only to realize that there is no expectational gap, and they just wasted two days. Still, there are a lot of things that can be done in a minimal amount of time.

CASE STUDY ON KNOWING THE BUSINESS

I discussed these themes with Alex, a brilliant portfolio manager who was very specific about the kinds of questions to consider when looking for a differentiated view from what others in the marketplace had developed and the kinds of considerations that were critical in determining whether there was indeed enough evidence to support further time and effort in investing in a particular idea.

Kiev: Can you expand on the kinds of work necessary to determine whether it is worth pursuing research in a particular idea? What do you think about before you begin digging in with traditional fundamental research?

Alex: The expectational gap is essentially the gap between the expectations that are being applied by the marketplace and what you perceive. The larger that expectational gap, and the better you can define what that expectational gap is, the greater the magnitude of what you'll get paid if you close that gap.

So, recognizing something is cheap or recognizing that something looks like a good investment isn't even close to enough. You have to articulate clearly why it's priced here and what has gotten it here. What specifically is the misunderstanding, and why do you think you're different? Then, how is it going to close?

This doesn't mean that if there is no expectational gap the idea won't work. It just means that the probability of getting paid for being correct is random. There are a lot of instances where we actually miss good investments, where there is no expectational gap.

I think for ideas that have greater than three-year time horizons, the concept of expectational analysis is much less relevant because the true fundamentals of the business will determine after three years what it is.

People have a natural tendency to think they're the first to know something. They actually don't think about how many other people have combed over this idea. What we really try to encourage and teach is this extremely high level of skepticism on what you are observing and sort of where you are when you are observing it.

K: Could you talk a bit about the process and the work techniques that you have learned that can decrease the time you need to spend on a phone with an analyst to measure what's changed or where the buildup is?

A: There seems to be this misconception in finance that the more work you do the more likely you are to make money in a stock. In some cases, this is true. In a lot of cases, it's not only wrong, it's actually worse because you become overconfident. You do an excessive amount of work, and you think you understand everything about the company, but you actually don't know a lot about the stock.

I sort of set out to build a new model that was predicated on efficiency and velocity and identifying the gating factors in an investment idea first. So, in some of our largest positions we had as much work done as any analyst or team for that name if we have a giant position. The difference is the order in which we did the work. I am not advocating shortcuts to understanding the ideas. I am just advocating a different order in which you do this. We focus on the gating items first and what will prevent us from doing an idea.

Then as you get more developed in the stock prices, you will realize there are a lot of other things you can do to alert you to how much potential expectational gap there is so that you can prioritize on what things you dig down first. If you were looking at a growth stock, its multiple is probably predicated on the size of its margins. The size of its top-line growth should then be the first thing you want to focus on. How does this multiple stay here? How does the top line grow higher than the rate that the market seems to price?

What exactly is the method by which the market is valuing this type of stock? Let me approach those levers first instead of focusing on things like the subsidiaries and the names of all the different people on the management team and what the board looks like. These are things where people used to brag to me about how much they knew about a company. They actually had no view on why it was worth investing in. I think there is a misconception about how much knowledge you possess and how likely you are to win.

It really comes down to isolating what the levers are in a story. What's going to drive the incremental appreciation or depreciation, depending on whether you are long or short? Figure out the best way to tackle those levers. Then, if you get past those gating items, you can focus on the other things that will allow you to sleep at night, like debt maturities and what the balance sheet looks like. Other issues are relevant over the long term but may not be so relevant when you are first figuring out whether you will invest.

K: What are some of the gating factors that you have come up with in the past year, or more specifically, what's relevant today?

A: Some of the simple gating factors are: the feasibility of putting the position on, how many dollars you are trying to make, how liquid the position is, what type of potential upside you could be playing for, what the total investment market the company is in looks like, basic expectational components, current sell-side readings, price targets, short interest, and price action.

These are all things that take ten to fifteen minutes to get a much sharper view on what the opportunity looks like.

K: As an investment?

A: It relates to the concept of *chunking*. A person who has never played chess looks at a chess board and sees a lot of pieces. A great master who looks at the same board in the middle of play immediately sees that there are only three or four possible moves to make.

Some of the less simple forms are some of the expectational components and recognizing how much upside we are actually potentially playing for. How many dollars can we make over what period of time? Apply a time-adjusted, expected-value framework over the idea and think about how that fits into the rest of the portfolio. An idea that takes three years that is going to make a hundred percent is obviously less of a good bet than an idea that takes one year to make a hundred percent. An idea that will make fifty percent over six months is still better than that. These are the things that I force myself to think about first.

Next are the more qualitative factors that most people fall back on. Is this a good company? Is this a good management team? These are things that are definitely relevant and important, but I think they take a back seat. A lot of people put the cart before the horse in those type of situations and get caught being long excellent companies. That is just priced far too expensive.

K: Do you have any data on how you have done with the expectational analysis in terms of results, whether there were numerous variables that supported your model?

A: Unfortunately, I would say it's probably more anecdotal. The problem is that expectational analysis is an art, and you can't necessarily quantify whether certain factors are better than others. A lot of it is feel, where you just kind of know based on how it's trading and how people are talking and sort of how variant the view is. I can tell you that I have been doing this style of approach for seven years now. The only data that I have is my track record.

It's just like playing poker. You know if you are dealt a pair of aces you are eighty percent likely to win, but sometimes you don't win. So, expectational analysis is just a probabilistic framework. It increases your probability of being right. There are plenty of times where everything lines up and it still doesn't work.

So, if I have an idea that I love, and everything lines up, I will make that position gigantic because the probability of my winning is very high. In other instances, where the idea is great but the expectational analysis is horrific, I simply either won't play it, or I will play very small because I just don't think the probabilities are on my side.

K: From my perspective, to be able to think this way requires an ability to think outside the box, to think in the nonconsensus way, to think of it without getting support from the rest of the world. It takes some kind of internal fortitude to be able to have confidence in that kind of unique view of the world.

A: I think the greatest difficulty I have had is getting others to accept that it's okay to pass on a stock that worked. That's the hardest thing to teach. People seem to have this relentless view that you need to be right a hundred percent of the time. At the end of the day, it's similar to card playing. There are going to be hands that you fold, that probabilistically don't make sense, but they might have won the pot. It doesn't mean you should have played that hand.

We will take a situation, and we will spend a lot of time on it, and it doesn't line up. I'll say, "You know what? This just doesn't line up. Let's not play it. Let's not focus on it. Let's not waste time on it." Then it will work, and I will never hear the end of it for two weeks. It doesn't mean that the process was wrong.

Few people price how much of a waste of time it is if that idea doesn't work. Very few people consider that. They consider the P&L. If I lose money, they consider that. What they don't consider is the opportunity cost of what happens if the idea doesn't work. You are stuck for a day or a week putting out that fire, figuring out what you got wrong, figuring out how to make it right. Not only could you have not lost the money, but you could have been focusing on something fresh or new. There are a lot of ideas that we come across that are just too difficult to handicap. You have to say, "I can spend a month on this and still not be that much closer to recognizing whether I am going to win." I try to teach that it's okay to do a week of work, write it up, and still say "No."

K: Can you explain the difference in contrarian versus variant view, and tell how all of this might affect trading in a volatile market?

A: I think *contrarian* denotes "going the other way" whereas *variant* doesn't necessarily mean you are directionally different. It just means you might be different on magnitude. So, if the Street thinks any growth stock is going to beat earnings that year by twenty percent, but you think you're going to beat by fifty percent, that is variant, but it's not contrarian. It's a magnitude difference versus directional difference.

As for the second question, I always go back to the simple analogies. Would you drive the same speed on the highway if it's sunny and clear versus if it's a blizzard? The answer is no. That's kind of how I view economic inflections. In economic inflections, I don't know what's going to happen. I just know that the roads are a lot less safe, and therefore, I am more likely to drive slower. I am less likely to take aggressive turns and make aggressive bets. I think the simple reality is just acknowledging that you are in a snowstorm. I think if you can do that you can save yourself a lot of angst.

There are various things that you can do to assess expectations after you have done the fundamental analysis so that you can determine the risk you are taking before earnings: sell-side analyses, estimates, evaluation, technicals, relative performance, negative sentiment, public, media exposure, insider activity, options activity, and macro factors. An assessment of these kinds of datapoints will give you a much better feel for what's in the stock and what the market is expecting.

Remember, the path to closing the expectational gap will not necessarily be filled with catalysts. It could be filled with lots of little things, even though none of those things in and of themselves are catalysts. Or you may have a situation where you have an event path that is very short and the catalyst is huge. In the simplest example, you might have a biotech stock where the main event is simply getting a drug approval. That path would be very clear.

CASE STUDY ON EXPECTATIONAL ANALYSIS

Greg is an aggressive high-risk-taker. He is inclined to keep barreling forward, and this shows up in his propensity to keep buying momentum in growth stocks. In this dialogue, I am discussing with Greg how he can develop a differentiated view and identify the path to getting paid. The dialogue outlines some critical points for understanding expectational analysis and the kinds of distinctions that a PM must make.

Greg: I have been trying to build concentrated positions to improve my profitability. Obviously, I am taking a lot more risk there. Basically, four names all went against me on the same day. What did I get wrong? They were all earnings-related calls. What I got wrong was the expectational side of the analysis. I was expecting that they would do badly, but the market didn't really appreciate that, and one stock went up twenty percent. A crowded position had become a consensus position, and I didn't realize that.

The other ones that went against me were situations where the EPS weren't great. They weren't big beats, but they were essentially in line or better. The stocks went down ten percent each.

Kiev: Is there any lesson to be learned from this?

G: The first lesson is that I am now set up. You know I have spent the last couple of days setting up an expectational model. All the warning signs were there; I kind of ignored them. I didn't have a systemized method to say, "That's a warning flag. Therefore, going into earnings I will not be long the stock." So, my first takeaway is that the way to make money in this business is to identify the biggest gap between your expectations of each return and the market's expectations of return. When you can say something is going to go a hundred percent, the market is going to go down a hundred percent, that's a huge gap that you have to exploit. That's where you make the most money.

The next issue is time. How quickly can you do it, and what are the catalysts that will appear in that time to close that gap? What I have done is to identify names that I think are great companies and that I think are doing really well. I think they are doing fantastic.

Next, I am considering what the market thinks about this. I have already gone out there and done the work. I like the company, so I think, "Oh, the market doesn't expect it. My position expectations are high in the market, or I have got to do better than the market." So I am actually picking situations where I am getting the right answer, but I am getting the market expectation wrong.

K: You are overestimating what you know relative to what the market already knows. The gap between what you know and what the market knows may have already closed a little bit. You may be getting confirmation from your own thesis, which increases your own conviction, but you're not really getting a handle on what it is that the market really knows by talking to other hedge fund guys or doing whatever is necessary to give you a better sense.

G: I think part of it is not getting enough read, but part of it is self-consciously ignoring the read—not being cautious enough about what the market's expectations are. What's really hard is to gauge market expectation. The only market expectation that is really easy to gauge lies on the extreme. Maybe if I identify those extremes I can find examples of the stocks that fit into those extremes and then develop my opinion about whether those stocks are accurate within my universe. If I find the ones that are lying at extreme market expectations, then I can think about developing an edge and a variant view.

K: Then you are going to have a bigger gap. I think if you look at various studies that have been done, you will find that when people play earnings they don't do as well as they think they will do. In fact, they lose money fifty percent of the time.

G: That's what has happened to me. I have played earnings. When I
     spot what I know is an expectational gap, then I am quite a bit
     smaller in the name because I don't have the work behind it. So
     when I have done the work, what I am doing is reengineering the
     expectational gap to make it look attractive when it's actually not.
     So I am bigger in the stocks where I have the lowest wedge between
     expectations and market expectations. I am smaller in the stocks
     where I believe this stock should really be down. There is no way it
     can go down much further. So I am just going to have a small long
     position going in and at that time do the work on it.

K: It may very well be that you want to spend a little more time doing
     some of this expectation work because you may be more familiar
     with that. That may be the twenty percent of information that gives
     you the eighty percent move.

     I talked recently to a hedge fund manager who told me that his
     new analysts tend to spend most of their time working on the infor-
     mation that is available but that is the least relevant. That's because
     they have the most confidence in that information. To play the game
     with an edge, you have to go with the information that is available
     but that is the most relevant, which may be more psychologically
     risky and less comfortable.

G: The challenge that I have is marrying the time-consuming nature
     of portfolio management with the time-consuming nature of being
     an analyst. If I want an edge, I have to spend a lot of time doing
     that analysis. I think that's what I realized more than anything. I
     am competitive, and I want to do well. I push myself to get more
     concentrated, to take bigger risks.

     I have a very specific process that I go through for the stocks.
     I go in, and I look at the market expectations on these five dimen-
     sions. I get an algorithm, and my experience tells me which stocks
     look the most overvalued. Then I go in and I do my own work and
     identify that gap and then think about the time rate of return and
     capital that's going to get me to close the gap. I am not going to
     make money unless my view is different from consensus.

K: You have to watch out for the trap of confirmatory bias, where you
     tend to see things that confirm what you already know and are not
     hearing it as clearly as you need to.

G: I think this process will enable me to improve my odds, not so much
     in terms of getting the calls right but in terms of the risk/reward. I

think it's going to soar when I have made the right call and only drop a bit when I make the wrong call. I think that's really the most important thing. If you can have five or ten percent down on your bad calls and a twenty, thirty, or forty percent upside on your good calls, you have really nailed it.

Actually, the win/loss ratio of most winning traders is closer to 1.5. So, it's not quite five down, twenty up. It's fifteen up and ten down. This is not unlike golf in the sense that you really have to master your own response to events. If you are getting too much information coming in and too many people are saying, "This is the way to do it," and so forth, that gets distracting. You get away from finding your own grip and your own rhythm. Ultimately, there is something to be learned about how individualistic the game is, but within the individualism of the game everybody has to deal with the same kind of issues. You just have to deal with them differently because you are wired differently. That's what is so challenging about it.

So, after defining the expectational analysis, you need to examine a number of critical elements of a trade in order to decide on your level of conviction. Conviction is the last part of the equation, and it means the probability of getting paid if you are right. A useful approach to this is to rank each of the following individual categories regarding your idea:

- Quality of Catalysts
- Quality of Price Target/Valuation
- Quality of Expectational Gap
- Quality of Timing/Event Path

You must also learn to uncover high-conviction ideas that may currently be hidden among the medium-conviction ideas. You can do this by constructing a list of criteria or a template to which you can compare such factors as timing, sentiment, valuation, and various catalysts. From this information, you can formulate a path to getting paid.

Raising Your Conviction

The following is a list of questions that one trader suggested considering in determining what additional work you need to do on your companies to raise your level of conviction.

Background:

- Why is the stock trading at its current price?
- What are the critical issues on which most investors are focused?
- What additional work can you do to bolster your understanding of the company, the sector, the competitors?

Thesis:

- What is your bet?
- What is your variant perception (thinking independently of the herd or consensus) or differentiated view?
- How does your thesis play out in revenues/EPS relative to consensus expectations?
- What is your edge?
- What more do you need to do to build your differentiated view?
- How much are you communicating with other sell-side and buy-side guys to prove to yourself that you are still ahead of the curve?

Price Target:

- How do you arrive at your target price (calculation–thought–effort)?
- What is your variant view on valuation?
- What is the downside if you are wrong?
- How do you get there?

Timing:

- When do you get paid?
- What are datapoints or events that will confirm/refute your thesis?

Upcoming Events:

- What are the upcoming events that could/should impact the stock over the time horizon of your investment thesis?
- How much more *digging* (work) can you do to bolster your differentiated view?
- As you reach different milestones, consider whether you want to build your position still further beyond 10 percent to 15 or 20 percent (risk).

Risks:

- What are the risks specific to this thesis?
- How much volatility can you tolerate?
- Have you factored liquidity constraints into your calculations?

Management Assessment:

- Does management have a track record of creating value for shareholders?
- Do they have skin in the game?
- What else do you know about management that strengthens your thesis?
- What other factors might you want to consider in evaluating management?

Conviction Level:

- On a scale of 1 to 10, how strong is your conviction level in the idea?
- What would you need to do/see to raise/lower your conviction level?
- How much more creative work can you do to bolster your conviction so that you can take an even larger position?

IDEA VELOCITY

Each position should have the work behind it that merits inclusion in the portfolio at a "minimum" position size. What is that minimum standard of work? It's embodied in the *idea template*. You should be able to articulate what's been driving the stock, your variant view for the situation, how that translates into your view on earnings and valuation compared to the implicit or consensus view, the event path that gets you there, and how much you are willing to risk. In particular, the focus on event paths is what separates the good idea generators from the great.

You could use baskets for hedging, but even there I believe that idea generation is where you create the value. Minimize the number of decisions (time) you need to spend on the hedging. Also, the positions that don't have enough liquidity to get bigger are probably not worth your time. You want to prove that you can effectively express your ideas via cash positions. Time-weighted return on your ideas is the key!

IDEA TIMING

Perhaps the most difficult aspect of developing an expectational analysis is looking for a timeline. Nevertheless, if you can quantify the amount of time you expect it will take to reach the upsides and downsides of your trade, you will be better equipped to manage the risk effectively.

Although there is no "right" way to make money, the best approach is one in which investment style and investment horizon are agnostic and where ideas are evaluated with different investment time horizons by calculating their time-adjusted expected value, which probability weights the upside and the downside, and the timing of the upside/downside. Goal-setting is important in that it helps relate the portfolio return objectives to the targeted rate of return for the ideas.

You can maximize capital efficiency by increasing positions only when there is an expectation of realization. Ask yourself, "*When* is the probability of being proven right or wrong the highest?" You can help answer this question by measuring the holding period, the winning percentage, and win–loss ratio. These provide insight into your efficiency at balancing idea selection with the timing of the capital commitment to the idea.

IDEA COMPLETION

Coming up with a variant perception and defining the expectational gap requires work. In order to give those ideas the decided conviction that you need to move upon them, a trader has to be willing to dig in and go the extra mile to find the information he needs.

"If you are going home with positions and own a stock overnight, you should know what is going on," said one trader. "If something comes out that was public and anticipated, and you are unaware of it, it is irresponsible and stupid."

Successful traders understand why businesses are durable and valuable and what events will unlock value in the stock. Beyond the variant view and the path to getting paid, it is critical to understand certain things about the business and the people involved in every trade. A successful trader will want to know why an industry exists, the history of the industry, the major players, the drivers of growth in the industry, and the barriers to entry to the business. He will want to understand the business model, whether the business is scaleable, how to leverage the business model in order to understand whether a company is going to be profitable, and why one company will achieve greater profits and higher multiples.

By taking a look at all your information and processing it into the big picture, you can make more informed decisions about your trades. The analytical effort should be to distill things to their essence and not be obfuscated by details.

One way of keeping your information in focus is to talk to the companies themselves or visit their stores and factories in order to find inefficiencies or information discrepancies that can be translated into trades.

Of course, getting more information sometimes means letting go of your ego long enough to admit that you don't know everything. It means not worrying about what other people will think and stepping up to the plate to say, "Wait a minute. I don't understand. What does this business actually do? Can someone explain the business process?"

Dennis, a hedge fund manager, used pharmaceutical benefit managers (PBMs) as an example. He explained that many people have a huge misperception regarding PBMs, believing that they are just some sort of middlemen "between the payers of healthcare, HMOs, and employers—like a leech on the system—and they just kind of did some bills processing and claims, and they negotiated some discounts from one drug provider to the patient, and they pocketed a bunch of money." Very few understand that there is within the organization of PBMs a "twenty-three-person medical clients board that is totally independent that determines medical equivalency for drugs and that the way that they make their money is by constantly finding these opportunities to establish medical equivalency—not only generics, but medical equivalency, because in some cases Drug A is much more effective than Drug B, but in other cases they are equally efficient. If the medical board, independent of cost, decides that these two are basically functioning the same in eighty percent of all cases and can identify what's different about the other twenty percent, then, as a front-line therapy, the employer could really determine on cost which one they are going to choose because they're medically equivalent."

The fact is, according to Dennis, that if traders didn't go the extra step they would never really know that information. They wouldn't know what a PBM does and therefore would not be able to recognize how it creates value. To make the most informed decision, the analyst needs to know as much about the company as the CEO and COO know.

The more you understand the business model, the more you can understand what it will take to make things work. The more you know, the better prepared you will be to talk to analysts about the companies they cover.

Beginning traders, however, often experience trepidation when doing this, fearing that they won't know enough to sound intelligent. To assist them, I asked one senior trader/analyst for a list of important questions to consider when talking to an analyst. A few of the more cogent questions he suggested were:

- What are the critical factors that make a stock attractive in this group?
- Are there seasonal trends in the stocks' performance?
- Are there key number releases that can influence short-term price action in the stocks?
- Can you give me a call when you get the raw data?
- What's the timeframe of your recommendations?
- Which of your buys have a chance of working this month? Which are second-halfers?
- How long have you been recommending this stock?
- What is the history of the booms and busts in this group over the past few years?

If you can find the answers to all of these questions, then you are well on your way to being able to understand the value of a company and how it may be trading in the marketplace. But you need more than one source of information about the company and more than one technique to value a company. You also need to know sales, earnings, cash flow, assets, and management. You must be able to analyze fundamentals and news events, predict how companies will respond to events, and keep track of events. You should have information about share price and share price movements, some understanding of the balance sheet and income statement, and the ability to make some assessment of the quality of a company. Over time, you should have some sense of:

Income Statement:
- Revenues
- Gross, operating, and profit margins
- Earnings per share
- Cost of goods sold
- Depreciation
- Amortization

Cash Flow:
- Cash flow
- Capital expenditure

Balance Sheet:

- Receivables
- Inventories
- Shareholder's equity
- Assets
- Liabilities

Estimates:

- Earnings
- Sales
- Margins

The most advanced traders will try to assess companies and determine how things will evolve and even how Wall Street analysts may be upgrading or downgrading company prospects. Anticipating what a Wall Street analyst might report gives the savvy trader an advantage so he can trade contrary to how he expects the Street to respond.

The master trader will pay attention to earnings announcements as well as the actions of the big "elephant" firms such as Morgan Stanley, Salomon Smith Barney, and Lehman, among others. He uses the order flow of the elephants to give him some indication as to how things are going.

THE PSYCHOLOGICAL DIMENSION

What differentiates expectational analysis and variant perceptions from the investigation of fundamental data alone is the ability a trader needs to discern psychological and sentimental factors that make stocks move beyond the conventional numbers. Instead of just considering the *whats* of the information, traders must also investigate the *whys*:

- **Pattern recognition:** Look for patterns in evaluating the value of data and making more accurate estimates.
- **Seek out mispricings:** Look for mispricings, disconnects, and other things that suggest that buying a company gives you a good shot at winning the bet in a reasonably well-defined time period.
- **Pay attention to emotions:** Recognize how much the market is based on irrational and emotional decisions and learn to appreciate

these tendencies by reading the chart action as well as by assessing the quality of information from suppliers, distributors, and others in the food chain.

The best traders are continually upgrading their interview skills and their ability to separate the wheat from the chaff and the truth from hyperbole when they interact with managements. To become skillful in getting information on the business and the numbers, traders have to know how to communicate in the appropriate way and with whom to communicate. They need to know the right questions to ask, when to ask them, and how to ask them. They need to know how to identify or at least suspect when they are being lied to and how to adjust the questions if the answers they are receiving don't seem to fit. A trader has to know how to recognize tidbits of information that may come up in the course of a conversation that could lead to a rare gem and how to dig further on-the-fly.

Most often, a trader has one hour to talk to someone about a company. If he spends half to three-quarters of that time discussing something that isn't very important in the grand scheme of things, he has wasted his time and blown a valuable opportunity to gain insightful information that may help him develop a variant perception.

"There are some other tools that you can use to help you gauge how mature people are on the inside," explains one trader.

If you are getting pitched to short it, or you are hearing about your buddies who are shorting it, or the sell-side is going out, if it's hard to borrow, if you have seen an unusual amount of put activity in the options market, that's usually an indication that people are getting bearish or trying to protect their gains. There is not a lot you can do.

Usually, when you do this enough you will start to develop a feel. Within five minutes you can tell if it's risky. Then you know, "Wow I think I need to do real work on this to decide if I want to hold this into earnings, or I don't think earnings is that significant. I am going to hang out." It's a basic rule of thumb. Any stock that's up thirty percent in a quarter after a huge beat probably means that a lot of people are watching. As long as your decisions over time are good and are handicapping reasonably over time, you will save yourself a lot of money.

Another important people factor is seeking out a variety of independent opinions. If one source gives you a certain piece of information or confirms a certain hunch you may have, that's great. But if you are able to talk to three different sources and they all give you basically the same story, that is *excellent*. Your confidence level has just been raised substantially. Obviously, the more sources you have, the better your chances.

Knowing what to ask, when to ask, and how to ask those valuable questions goes back to the research process: how you are preparing for the interview itself.

CASE STUDY ON COMMUNICATING EFFECTIVELY

I had an opportunity to talk to a major hedge fund manager about how he and his team of analysts prepared for company meetings.

Kiev: How do you strategize before meeting with management?

Pruitt: We look at it, and we see these datapoints. We put them together, and then we go company by company. We ask ourselves, "How much is this company doing well or poorly?" When the industry conditions return back to normal without these inventory drawdowns or merger destructions or other kind of transitory effects, what will the numbers look like then? So that's going to help us create a variant perception versus what the Street thinks. This is quite different from what the Street does, which is generally to take the last two datapoints and extrapolate, and if it's growth it's going to grow that way.

Then we are having the conversation with management to try to figure out whether we see this business resuming in a nine-to-twelve-month period. Is that consistent with your framework? Why do you think that? Fine; well, you say that your business is down because of these destructions. Let's try to add up how much that has really been. Maybe your business is down in front of the reasons. Maybe you are losing shares and you have bad products, maybe bad capital allocations. So, we are using those hour-long meetings to try to confirm whether we believe management understands and is confirmatory or there are other things going on.

K: You really have to know the company pretty well to be able to ask management these kinds of questions.

P: There is no such thing as generic questions. We had a call last week where we were talking with the management of XYZ. They just had great numbers; they came in at eighty-seven cents. The Street was at eighty-one cents. They guided up for the year. The stock traded down by four percent, because even though they had great numbers overall (from an earnings perspective), one of the key ratios showed that there was a little bit of pricing competition in commercial business. Government business did better and more than upsided, but everybody is worried about competitively how's that going? We started talking to investor relations. I saw the questions, but the problem was the tone in which my analyst started to go after IR. The investor relations guy immediately became defensive. All he wanted to do was say, "Look, our numbers are great. The Street is wrong. We are sick of short-term investors. They can't see it. We can't explain it." All he wanted to do was rant and vent his frustration.

K: Did he really understand the questions?

P: He understood the questions, but he was beat up. So, I took over the call, and I changed it to, "We're your friend. It says we own two million shares. We own ten million shares. It hasn't been updated yet. We are the sixteenth largest shareholder. You don't have to tell us about the short-term-oriented nature of the market. We know the short-term inclination of the market. We know your franchise is worth more than the last sale. We know that the market is misinterpreting it. So, I am sure you are going to have to make this speech a thousand times. At least now you can make it nine hundred and ninety-nine. You don't have to get flustered because we share that. What we want to figure out is, the people who are looking at the wrong measure, at what point and time are they going to figure out that it is the wrong measure or that the wrong measure is going to turn positive, anyway, such that the true value of the company can be recognized?"

Immediately he is disarmed. Now he doesn't think it's adversarial. He is not defensive. At least we can talk substantively about the real issues, what's really behind the pricing issues, and it turns out it's a mixed business. They are losing some smaller accounts because of the reputation issues they had because of the options investigation they had a year ago, which we knew was a risk long end for a one-year period of time. Then that's very profitable business. On that thesis, we are long at twelve times earnings on 2008. The company has overcapitalized. They are buying back stock. If it was 2011 or 2012, I am not sure we would have the patience, but its 2008; we can sit around for twelve months. Hopefully, it takes only four months for people to recognize that this is really what's going on. We can do that.

So, as I said, I wish I could say here is the critical insight that we have developed over the years. It's literally all these pieces of the mosaic and putting them all together.

K: I have never heard it quite as crystal clear as you have just described it in terms of the depth of understanding of the whole process.

P: If we were going to come to you to say, "Look, our organization has a problem. Our hedge fund is not working. The symptoms are people are unhappy and morale is low. Turnover is high. Our performance is a wreck," okay, you now know the couple of surface bullet-point things. In order to give us the best advice, what would you do? You wouldn't just talk to one person; you would talk to all the people. It could be that you know the diagnosis, that you may actually have talked to somebody for three or four hours. But, it would be very different if had you spent two days and talked to everybody. You'd get a much more complete picture. What's the variant perception? The variant perception is that we are doing a lot more work than most people who are trying to make a diagnosis.

In sum, Pruitt is emphasizing the need to do differentiated work to establish the variant perception from the rest of the players in the marketplace, which gives him a huge edge in his investment approach. Beyond this thorough study of the mosaic, he also focuses on understanding the opposite opinion (the bear case if he is bullish, the bull case if he is bearish), and in this Socratic way he digs even deeper to understand the strengths and flaws in his investment thesis. This takes great confidence and humility.

In order to get the information you need, you may have to seek it from people with whom you don't normally coordinate efforts. If you need the information and there is someone with more experience who can answer your questions, don't be afraid to ask. You want to know the opposing case.

You want to know the drivers. Presumably, everybody knows the fundamentals. What's really critical is knowing what the gap is between what you know and what's potentially in the stock, where it's going to be in three months or six months. That gap is based on behavioral economics, game theory, sentiment, all kinds of things over and above the fundamentals.

Talk to your team about your ideas. Present your information, your ideas, your variant perception, your conviction, and your plan. Then, listen to and answer their questions. One trader described how an investment committee at his firm reviewed all ideas together. While the committee consisted of only four or five of the most senior people in the firm, they covered a range of different industries. The trader explained that the benefit to this committee was in its diversity. Each person represented a different mindset, a different type of knowledge in which the ideas presented could be reviewed.

Sometimes, hashing it out with a team brings questions to the surface that you might not have considered, either adding to your conviction level or sending you back to the drawing board to dig a little deeper. Sometimes, you will find that a teammate has already done work in that area or a similar area and has valuable insight. Sometimes, someone who is involved in a totally different industry will offer a bit of information that will trigger a brainstorm.

With that being said, remember this. While it's always nice to have the opinions of peers, trusted confidants, and advisors, in the end, you alone are responsible for the decision you make. You must be the strategic thinker, and sometimes you have to follow your gut instinct. To do this successfully, you must also learn to manage your own emotions and decision-making processes.

 CHAPTER IN REVIEW

1. It is crucial to understand the variety of factors (outside of fundamentals) that play a role in determining stock prices. In order to make money in the markets, a trader needs to know something that other people don't know yet.

2. The strategic trader is someone who can "think outside the box," someone who will be comfortable dealing with unprovable events or the tails of events rather than having to rely on consensus or conventional ways of approaching problems.

3. The key to thinking creatively is to look for inefficiency in the market and to focus more on issues of psychology, game theory, and behavioral finance than on fundamentals. Ideally, you should develop a differentiated view and decipher the data to determine which trades have the most potential before investing a large percentage of time investigating them.

4. The best way to make money in the markets is to know something that others don't yet know, to think ahead of the curve, and to anticipate when something is going to happen. The more you know, the more you can make a calculation about the likely target or trajectory the stock is going to follow because you have done the work. The objective is to do research that supports a variant perception in terms of where a stock is and where you expect it will be when its full value is realized.

5. The larger the gap between where the price is and where you expect it to be, once value is unlocked, the more profit you can make. The clearer and shorter the event path, the more likely you are to get paid if you are right. The better you can articulate that gap and the more research and tools you can apply to determine the path to getting paid, the more you can expect to make.

6. In order to think strategically you have to consider how you construct an idea, take into consideration the velocity and timing of your idea, and learn how to tie all your information together in order to complete the idea and bring it to successful fruition.

7. Instead of just considering the *whats* of the information, traders must also investigate the *whys*. To become skillful in getting information on the business and the numbers, traders have to know how to communicate in the appropriate way and with whom to communicate.

8. While it's always nice to have the opinions of peers, trusted confidants, and advisors, in the end, you alone are responsible for the decisions you make. You must be the strategic thinker.

CHAPTER 5

Separating Emotions and Decisions

The Ability to Be Self-Aware

I n the late 1970s, I was invited to join the U.S. Olympic Sports Medicine Committee, which opened up to me the amazing world of high-performance athletic competition. In my work with a wide variety of Olympic athletes, I learned about the power of explicit goal-setting and techniques of visualization, relaxation, and meditation for enhancing gold medal performance.

During my Olympic committee work, I learned that those who made the Olympic team, and especially those who made it to Olympic gold, had been visualizing these achievements for years. They allowed the vision and commitment to the result and faith in their eventual success to support their efforts through many years of hard work, failure, and challenge. In particular, a proactive strategy gave these athletes the confidence to embrace their fears and associated emotional responses to the stress of high performance, thereby converting the anxiety of the fight-or-flight stress response into a positive, adaptive approach to the situations they faced.

While teaching these principles to others in intensive weekend Life Strategy Workshops during the 1980s, one participant sought out my advice about applying these techniques to the trading arena. As I told him then, and have since reiterated countless times in my books and training seminars, the key to trading success is to promise or commit to a stretch target over a specified time horizon and then construct a strategy to reach this target. This can be accomplished by learning good risk management principles, developing a solid research process to understand the fundamentals of the companies, and then monitoring performance. As easy as this may sound, it is not particularly easy to implement, especially in turbulent times when traders are feeling very stressed and pulled out of their game.

CASE STUDY ON THE EMOTION OF DRAWDOWNS

The following dialogue with Nathan illustrates how one portfolio manager has learned to understand the balance between emotions and risk management and to take an offensive approach to profitability. Here, he demonstrates how an experienced PM can weather a market downturn and major drawdown. He shares the lessons he has learned on how to deal with cautiousness and how to develop confidence from his process as well as the struggles of other emotional underpinnings in his overall strategy.

Nathan: We last spoke when I was through my stop levels and the market and positions forced me to take something off the table.

Kiev: Giving up potential opportunities?

N: It was necessary. I had to be responsible for my positions as we discussed last time; sometimes the market can stay irrational longer than you can stay solvent.

K: The psychological tension of managing a portfolio?

N: Correct.

K: Did you get back in?

N: I just reduced risk. What I had remaining in those positions made money back, and I was adding to other types of trades with the theme that if that was the bottom, then there was recovery to be had. I probably made back fifty percent of my losses, and where I am right now there is breathing room to be offensive and have an opinion on where the market is going. I am reestablishing some of those views.

K: What has to take place for that transition to occur, where you go from being defensive to being offensive? How do you know?

N: It's a combination of two things. First, you have a view of the market, and when it is not going in your favor and you are losing money every day, you are not supposed to fight the tape. You are supposed to recognize that there may be too many people like you out there, or there may be a flaw in your analysis. But, as you become successful in your view and start making money, and the market is doing things that you consider rational, you get more confident to add to your trade and believe your view and how the price reaction should be appropriate, and you will start to make money.

K: When you see that it builds your confidence?

N: There are three things that build your confidence. One is your P&L and proof in the pudding that you are making money because of your view and can add to your view and hopefully get to your target. The other aspect is discrete events in the market that add or subtract from your confidence level.

The third aspect of what we do for a living is fundamental news. Depending on the outcomes of these three events, it will determine how big I want to be in my current position in trading interest rates and where I think the next trade is.

K: Are some people so traumatized by negative events that they don't have the cool or calm to rely on their fundamentals?

N: Yes. People get sticker shock. When you lose as much money as people have lost recently, they are hesitant to get back in. They are less aggressive. They tend to buy bad levels.

K: Then they chase it?

N: Yes. They start chasing it, and you are buying bad levels, and the market forces those people out of the trade, and it works its way into the next trade. The market is ahead of itself; then it will back up and then move forward.

I have to be responsible to the portfolio and not stubborn to my view. You need to have the confidence that you are doing well, and when you have that you can't just do thirty percent of what you need to do. You have to be able to jump back in. That is the big game I am playing now.

K: Has your ability to do that changed?

N: Yes. I used to be very loss conscious. I did not maximize gains. Now I am not trying to make up for the losses; you can't ever

do that. If I am right, I expect to make a certain amount of dollars as opposed to being right and not losing a certain amount
of money. The battle I am playing with now is if I am right, how
much am I supposed to make in this trade? If I make a third
of that, I should be disappointed in not performing up to my
expectations, which is the philosophy I started with last year
when we started talking.

K: Do you have to push yourself to do this?

N: Yes, I have to push myself. I am getting into positions bigger than
what I would usually do. In the past, I would look at my delta and
say, "That's enough." Now, I say, "That's not enough." If we go to
a price level, I need to be sized a certain size to get to that price
level with a backdrop of where I am in my P&L cycle because
of the big drawdown of two weeks and to make sure I don't get
to that position again where I can't trade offensively. It's a very
fluid situation.

K: The waves are crashing, and you have to keep forging ahead.

N: Two weeks ago, I was disappointed that I couldn't do what I
wanted to do because I was being responsible. I lost enough
money to say there is a greater force in play; I need to risk manage the portfolio. Now I am able to fight the good fight again. I
feel better that I can now trade offensively.

Nathan's process has taken some time to develop and has required the
development of a lot of objectivity about his own emotional responses and
a commitment to learning to handle the discomfort associated with playing
to win. As this dialogue illustrates, this is an ongoing process and takes
continual coaching to help the PM realize his full potential.

As Nathan just illustrated, success in trading, as in other high-
performance tasks, requires the ability to master fear and other emotional
and behavioral responses to stress so that fund managers can develop
workable processes for profitable results in the face of the uncertainty,
change, and complexity of the markets. This means learning to manage the
stress of the markets, drawdowns, and the challenges associated with commitment to outsized results by stretching oneself and entering the zone of
discomfort, which is a prelude to extraordinary performance. Therefore, a
portfolio manager is ultimately the instrument of his own success and must
learn to read his own emotional and psychological signals as well as those
of others in the game.

THE SOURCE OF FEAR

The body's response to stress is meant to be adaptive, helping you to cope with dangerous situations. It prepares you for *fight*—stand your ground— or *flight*—flee the situation—by increasing blood flow to the muscles, increasing heart rate and breathing rate, emptying the stomach and gastrointestinal tract of blood, and heightening your senses. Physiologically, when you become anxious or fearful, your heart pumps adrenaline into the bloodstream, a natural or automatic response to danger, novel stimuli, or symbolic risks. Thus, you may experience palpitations and difficulty breathing. Dizziness, lightheadedness, difficulty swallowing, and butterflies in your stomach are also common accompaniments of the adrenaline response.

These symptoms often burst forth in the fast-paced world of trading. They might be a response to the stresses of business or to memories of past trading experiences, not to actual danger. Regardless, your body reacts the same. It becomes overloaded. Your capacity to cope effectively is significantly reduced by the overreaction of your nervous system. You expend excess energy to reduce these reactions or to hide or control them. And if you don't recognize that this is happening and don't attempt to deal with these responses, you are likely to become overwhelmed. Therefore, to manage anxiety and fear while dealing with the uncertainty of the market, you need to be able to notice and separate your emotional responses from the decisions that you are making.

Because it is natural to want to be in control, you may try to react to stress by trying to reject these feelings or, in another control attempt, you may tighten or tense up your body even more. It doesn't work. The adrenaline keeps on pumping. As you deny your responses instead of owning them or letting them pass, your stress level tends to increase rather than decrease. Your anxiety escalates. Rather than recognize and heed your body's signals by slowing down, resting, relaxing, and regrouping so that you can accurately assess and handle the reality before you, you are caught between the escalation of symptoms that you cannot deny and your need to stay in control.

The more panicky you feel, the less willing you are to let go and allow yourself to experience the feelings. Under this increasing amount of stress, it becomes impossible or near impossible for you to relax and to allow the waves of adrenaline to course naturally through your body. Rather than going with the flow, you are likely to identify the anxiety with the *origin* of the stress and then assiduously learn to avoid any activity that awakens that memory. Then, your anxiety-reducing rituals or compulsions become even more debilitating than the original anxiety.

This happens especially when someone has been losing money and is in negative P&L territory. Such was true for Merl, a relatively new PM, who had little experience with market downturns and a distinct tendency to blame the risk manager or management rather than face up to the difficulties that he had been having with his trading. His denial of responsibility and projection of blame onto others often showed up in his meetings with investors.

During difficult market periods, traders find all sorts of things to blame for their poor performance. They blame other unresolved projects that they find distract them from focusing on their portfolios. They are more sensitive to rumors about changes in the firm direction and express concerns as to whether certain strategies will be eliminated going forward. This is accentuated by the fact that in times of drawdown and greater volatility, consulting firms are brought in to examine ways of improving strategies going forward, and this creates a certain amount of anxiety in people who are already anxious.

Some traders, such as Joe, manage the greater volatility and rise to the occasion, finding new opportunities. Joe was feeling very confident after a credit crisis had calmed down. He was looking to diversify his bets out of U.S. rates and to do some European rates and currency trades. While he was not bullish, he was somewhat positive about how things were setting up and certainly thought we had passed the major crisis point and that there was a lot more confidence at the moment in the stability of the banking system since the problematic issues had been identified. He admitted that we were not out of the woods, but there was more clarity and confidence.

Others like Keith, who was up about $40 million, were also very positive about the markets. He recognized that more effort was needed to find good ideas and started coming in early and doing a lot more work. He consciously took advantage of the panic in the markets and the inclination of everyone to get out of trades. The key seemed to be to focus on the process and not be distracted by the emotionality around him.

Of course, tuning out the emotions of everyone around you is not necessarily a good idea. As Donovan suggested, sometimes the emotions are a clue as to what is going on. Whereas it's important to stay focused on your own process, it is often difficult to know whether you are too early or too late; therefore, there is some value in paying attention to the emotionality of the markets.

CASE STUDY ON TRADING STRESS

In early May 2008, a new PM sent me an e-mail asking to meet with me to discuss job stress and how he could mitigate the emotional factors. When we sat down to talk, I asked him to tell me a little bit about his issues.

Kiev: What has been stressful for you?

Stan: This is my first year as a PM. I am finding it very stressful.

K: In what way?

S: Physically. I am trying to get to the gym. I am drinking less. My upper back is tense. I am more tired at the end of the day. I am cognizant of trying to be good at my job. Ninety-five percent of it is making unemotional decisions, but the stress is bringing emotion into my decision-making process. If I am down on a particular day, I am hesitant to make a move, to buy another stock, even if I have done all the necessary work to give me a lot of conviction. If one stock is blowing up on me, and I see an opportunity, say something is massively oversold or overbought, or a short squeeze that would be great to short, I second-guess myself.

K: Your decision making isn't as crisp when you are feeling stressed out.

S: I'm hesitant for fear I might be wrong. When I am wrong in my portfolio, I start to second-guess other decisions that I make. Probably the converse is true. When I am doing really well, I make mistakes the other way, feeling overconfident. Last year, as a check, I had my manager review all my positions. I had an excellent year last year [2007]. I might have been more inclined to make those decisions because I had backup and reassurance. I felt overconfident about those decisions because he was there as a gate. It's helpful to have someone to talk to.

K: Talking about stress or portfolio management or a mixture of both?

S: I guess a mixture of both. How do I mitigate the stress and separate it from my decision-making process?

K: Let's pick one of the things that you don't know what to do about, something that is creating stress for you, to see if we can handle it.

S: I'm down seven million dollars year-to-date on one-hundred-fifty million dollars allowable gross. I am using about fifty percent. I had a big blowup and took my gross down from one-hundred-fifteen million to eighty million. Some positions worked out, and I sold some of those longs. It's not a good performance, three down months and one up, really volatile both ways. So, I see trading opportunities, and I have been avoiding them. I am afraid to step in.

K: Do you know those stocks?

S: Yes.

K: Take one.

S: ABC reported a fine quarter, but the CEO at the opening of the call made some comments that a couple of businesses were weak, which accounted for two percent of revenues, and the stock sold off six percent. It was already pretty cheap. This was going to close flat; we're up.

K: It was as far down as you could go?

S: Yes.

K: You wanted to buy it?

S: It went down to fifty-two and change. I had real underperformance in my portfolio that day.

K: So, you see this opportunity but are hesitant to take it. Would it be a high-conviction idea?

S: Yes.

K: Where did it go?

S: Today it's at fifty-eight, a week later, ten percent in four trading sessions. Today I saw an opportunity and took advantage of it.

K: Did you have some low-conviction ideas that you could have gotten out of in exchange for these higher-conviction ideas?

S: Not really. I tend not to be a trader. I typically don't take advantage of stuff. I am really deep. I get my path. It is typically not a week. Most of my stuff I like for six months or a quarter. It's not often that I have a trade. I have enough capital to be getting these.

K: How many opportunities have you missed?

S: Five really good ones, probably about ten all together. I've gotten involved a bit but not enough to make a difference.

K: Have you tracked their performance after you failed to get in to see how much you would have made? If you missed a lot of actual P&L

opportunities, you will eventually convince yourself of the value of incrementally getting more involved, that these aren't flyers. You want to monitor the performance of not buying these stocks. What is the value of *not* buying these stocks? You should build a database of these stocks so you can see what you are missing.

S: That's a great idea.

K: You need to monitor your own behavior to see what can be tweaked. Your issues will be particular to you. Some of the stress is because you are indecisive; that creates anxiety.

It's a good idea to be proactive in managing your drawdown, reaching out to risk management for advice on how to manage your book. It's probably a good idea to try to push your mentor to be more critical about your portfolio management. Most mentors seem to be very diplomatic and hands-off. You have to take it upon yourself to ask for more critical comments and guidance and suggestions about how to incrementally get bigger and take advantage of opportunities, if only for short periods of time. The risk managers may help with this, as can your mentor and some of the other PMs with whom you talk.

Stan's reactive and cautious pattern is reflective of his inexperience. As he develops into a master trader he will develop the ability to do more of what he is starting to do now—self-assessing, seeking coaching, and learning not to be thrown by his emotional reactions. Eventually, he will be able to reach a centered state where he is able to see the movement of the market without becoming reactive to it.

SELF-ESTEEM AND SELF-DISCIPLINE

When a trader reacts to his emotions, he often tricks himself into believing false notions about himself and his abilities. Because of a lack of information or an inability to correctly assess the information he has, he either overvalues his abilities—thinking he is far better at certain tasks than he really is—or he undervalues his potential—falling prey to insecurities and poor self-esteem. A trader who is able to observe his own emotions without reacting to them has to have both self-discipline and good self-esteem.

Self-discipline is the ability to do what needs to be done to enhance one's skills. It is an inner capacity to plan and organize one's time, to develop one's skills, and to maximize one's conditioning without the need for external monitoring. Self-esteem, on the other hand, is the confidence to achieve the goals one sets.

As self-esteem diminishes, the ability to take criticism is reduced, and each criticism is viewed as a personal attack. This inability to deal with failure simply confirms one's doubt about oneself. Since trading inevitably involves failure, a healthy self-esteem often differentiates the individual who will grow from the individual who will crumble in the face of defeat. An individual with good self-esteem will rebound from failure, often seeing a missed shot or a blown trade simply as a challenge to win at the next opportunity.

A direct benefit of positive self-esteem is the ability to make good decisions. A successful trader will have the ability and willingness to make instant decisions and to function, to some degree, on instinct.

Regardless of how much coaching a trader receives, when it comes down to day-to-day trading, he must react instantly. He cannot be guilty of "paralysis through analysis." Thus, I look at decision making as the willingness to act quickly and to risk making an occasional error in so doing.

Of course, part of developing this type of decision-making ability involves acquiring intelligence and knowledge to make those decisions overall correct ones. So, self-esteem cannot really be separated from decision making. In order to be willing to risk—in order to be willing to be wrong on occasion, to make a mistake, to look badly—an individual's self-esteem must be sufficient to allow this.

The self-confident trader also isn't afraid to stand up for what he wants when he believes in his abilities. For example, Eric had an enthusiastic desire to move to Hong Kong to take advantage of the trading hours, access to managements, and the anticipated continued boom in Chinese and Asian stocks. At the time he thought we were in the third year of a ten-year upward cycle and that there were huge opportunities as China built out its infrastructure. As a trader, he ran with 19 percent NMV against his GMV and was good at taking both NMV and GMV down when necessary. The previous year, he was running $25 million NMV against a BP of $150 million or 16.6 percent. He had been trading Asia for 14 years and thought he had another 14 years to devote himself to this effort. He believed so much in the move that he was willing to incur some of the costs involved. His confidence helped him approach management and present a convincing case for his move.

Of course, there are times when that kind of self-confidence can be mistaken for arrogance. But, a healthy self-esteem is very different from a false sense of bravado. A self-confident person has no trouble admitting his mistakes. While he is confident in his abilities, he is fully aware that he is not perfect. An arrogant trader, on the other hand, often covers up his insecurities and is very reluctant to admit his own faults. His underlying fears of failure and looking badly may, therefore, keep him from taking an honest look at his trades and learning from his mistakes.

So, the process of self-awareness and self-examination is continuous. It requires a willingness to hear the opinions of others regarding your work, to take an honest, hard look at the facts, and to sometimes revisit earlier-learned lessons and recommit to original strategies of winning.

For example, Will is a PM who was losing money and had to realize through coaching conversation that he was trading not to lose. His trades were being based on an underlying need to maintain an image rather than trading to win in terms of a goal. Because Will remained very coachable, he was not resistant to suggestions that he needed to shift gears. He did not become defensive or try to support his losing approach. After some time of reflection, he realized that he might be rationalizing his inclination to hold onto his positions because of the sunk-costs fallacy, which was making him miserable, and that the wiser strategy would be to reformulate his approach based on his targets for the year and to ask questions about where his assets might be more profitably employed while waiting for these mergers to occur. He began to look for other opportunities and slowly take down his losing positions to stop the persistent bleeding.

Through this process of self-examination, Will discovered that he was too concerned with changing his mind about positions he had advocated and looking like he no longer had conviction in something in which he once believed. He had to address whether he was more concerned about his public image or his profitability. He recognized that if he was truly interested in profitability, the logical course of action would be to admit to the fact that he may have been wrong in the timing and find better places for deploying his capital.

Like Will, traders who have developed both the self-discipline and the self-esteem that lead to success are in essence very coachable. They accept direction, change behaviors that impact performance, and use their intelligence to learn and grow rather than defend preconceptions and old habits. The successful trader has a sense of urgency about producing results and the willingness to commit to stretch goals on targets. He has a high degree of ego strength and resilience and the ability to rebound from repeated failures.

LEARNING FROM DRAWDOWNS

The loss of money in a market downturn often sets in motion a progressive development of such symptoms as psychological numbing, decision paralysis, and even confusion in some PMs who become trapped in their losing positions and unable to act as rationally as they can under normal circumstances. Therefore, the ability to self-assess after periods of drawdown demonstrates great self-awareness, lack of defensiveness, and willingness to change and to listen to coaching recommendations—all signs of someone with the capacity to adapt and win.

On the other hand, the highly stressed PM may find that his ability to make sound and timely decisions has been impaired so that he holds onto losing positions at a time when he ought to be delevering his book and reducing risk. Instead, he is rationalizing his decision to hold on as a good buying opportunity. He may be more suggestible to rumors and may find himself reacting excessively to the stressfulness of the markets as well as to his own stress. He begins to take more reckless positions than he might have in the past. While getting bigger in a losing position may be a sound decision, it must be carefully weighed; and you want to be able to hear the thoughtfulness behind the decision and not simply accept knee-jerk rationalizations as sufficient. Basically, the less skilled or experienced manager doesn't have a process, holds onto his losers, chases flyers, overreacts to the market drawdown or gets paralyzed, rationalizes his performance, justifies, gets irritated, and is avoidant. In addition, he often mistakes good results in good times for skill, and is highly susceptible to hubris, overconfidence, and excessive emotional panic. He lacks discipline, gets emotionally attached to positions, and forms conclusions based on faulty notions.

Anne is an example of a trader who demonstrated the ability to learn from past mistakes and devastating drawdowns. After a PM review in January, it was evident that she had clear-cut improvement since the previous

February, when she had experienced a big drawdown. She is now managing her book with longs and shorts balanced, running neutral, good on the short-side and hedging with alpha shorts and options. Her liquidity profile has improved. When ideas are good, she presses her bets. When they go wrong, she cuts her positions and manages her drawdowns extremely well.

She is pleased to be running $250 million and hopes that by the end of the year she will have demonstrated good portfolio management skills, the ability to handle her nets commensurate with her GMV, good teamwork, and the ability to manage her analysts and expand her sector coverage from consumer staples and retail to gaming and lodging. She believes that she could run $500 million by adding five to ten more large-cap names with the aid of an analyst.

By reviewing her trades, Anne was able to correct her errors in managing her portfolio and improve her overall performance by becoming more hedged and balanced. This kind of tolerance for failure and the capacity to reassess and recover after adversity are major characteristics of the successful trader.

CASE STUDY ON SELF-ASSESSING DURING DRAWDOWNS

In the summer of 2007, many traders began to create doomsday scenarios in their minds or listen too assiduously to the Cassandras of doom who populated the airways. As the drawdown continued, the sense that it would never end kept coloring the interpretation of events. I spoke with Terrance about how he handled the drawdowns that came in the fall of 2007. I also explored ways in which he and his investment team managed changes in their portfolio.

Terrance: First of all, risk management happens before you enter the crisis. By the time you are in the middle of the crisis, you are messed up. So, it's always the right thing to do to take a fraction and consider it. Let's not worry about what we thought before; let's just worry about what we think right now. Let's not worry about whether we are up three or down three or whether we are having a good year or a bad year; let's just look without bias, without hope, without emotion. Let's just refresh everything we know. Let's really look at the merchandise and think, "Will we have this exact same position size today?"

The definition of *insanity* is doing the same thing over and over again expecting it to come out differently.

Kiev: I think Einstein said that.

T: You go through contingency plans, but there are two types of emergencies—ones you have drilled on and ones you haven't drilled on. We have done this drill before. This was one where there is a fire in a building; you know what to do. On this one, we are confident. We have run our scenarios. What if the market has a liquidity crisis? What if there is an economic scare? What if there is a mortgage scare? Because we were short mortgages, we knew that there was a chance there was a mortgage scare. We already knew the *what-if*. I think we were just mentally prepared for it a little bit.

K: This sounds very interesting. Can you expand a bit more on how you integrate this analysis into your process?

T: Part of the culture is not only to go through the eighty-percent cases but go through the twenty-percent cases in advance to try to think down the decision tree. Well, if *this* happens, how will we react and what will we do? If a fire alarm goes off and you have done fire drills, you call me, and we move to the nearest exit, and it's not a big deal. If you have never done that before, you are scared and you are running around like a chicken with your head cut off. So, I think culturally we are well prepared. Number two is you gain confidence as a team. Any one person in a crisis is going to get a moment of dollar panic. If you publicly submit it to this good process of being prepared and going through this kind of what-if discussion, then by definition you will have a more orderly reaction during times of market disorder and market crisis. I think that's true no matter what the nature of the emergency.

K: Sounds very much like what good coaches do—review the game films to see what happened and how to improve performance.

T: People who have gone through the process of thinking about it, assessing it, and drilling out things, the depth is there.

Yeah, it's about drawing on your past experience, but I think culturally we analyze our mistakes. People who don't analyze their mistakes repeat them.

K: So, what are some of your mistakes?

T: One of our mistakes is changing our minds just because of the conditions of the marketplace. We didn't want to live with that discomfort or shame of owning a stock that is down for a period of time. That willingness to look at our mistakes and run from them has been helpful.

K: Is it fair to say that a large number of firms don't think that way?

T: Yes, a lot of people running money don't because it's hard to do, and there is timing. It requires personnel continuity, and it requires your own intellectual honesty, and those things are hard to find.

In essence, Terrance is talking about the value of preparing for a variety of eventualities and being prepared for dealing with the black-swan or tail-end events, which are potentially catastrophic and which, from the summer of 2007, roiled the financial markets in a very dramatic and unpredicted way. All of this has to do with learning to be comfortable with the uncomfortable.

GETTING COMFORTABLE WITH THE UNCOMFORTABLE

As contradictory as it sounds, in order to truly learn from drawdowns and to master your trading experiences, you have to learn how to be comfortable with being uncomfortable. Self-awareness alone is not enough. Sometimes traders are aware of their errors but unwilling to do anything about them.

For example, George is a trader whose excessive caution prevents him from being as big as he can be. His plan for this year has been to get a list of names and target prices from the sell-side, have a goal of $1 million per month with the use of $20 million of capital, and improve on his portfolio management. He is very good about getting out of losing positions and has good statistics to show for it, although last year he missed some upside moves after getting out of positions and not getting back in when the stocks moved up again.

He recognizes that he needs to do more on the short side than he has done in the past, but has yet to develop any ideas about how he would do this or how to provide incentives to other guys in the firm to trade more on the short side. We discussed the fact that it takes more effort on the short side to do the work to get at structural alpha shorts than comparable trades on the long side, which may be one reason why people don't trade on the short side. Basically, George is too risk averse and is aware of it; however, he seems unable to face his fears. Self-awareness, then, must be coupled with a willingness to get into the discomfort zone if it is to have any value.

True knowing is not emotional but intellectual. Attachment to ideas based on how we feel is a primary source of confusion, because our feelings are always subject to contradiction and doubt. Our emotions give us frozen views of reality. We rely on what we feel rather than what we know. The truth is in the realm of the known, the reality, and then we overlay an emotional component on top of it and try to manage the resulting thoughts. Stress, then, comes from the emotional overlay on top of the experience.

CASE STUDY ON BEING COMFORTABLE WITH DISCOMFORT

In this interview, I am talking with Randy, a seasoned portfolio manager with whom I have been working for several years. He is extremely conscientious and always eager to learn more about how to handle his emotions so as to improve the efficiency of his trading and portfolio management. Here he illustrates that mastering one's emotions is critical and not an impossible feat, even in the most difficult of times.

Kiev: I have been talking to a whole bunch of people. The macro factors are roiling the markets, and you have to get the events right in your assessment. If you get the events wrong, you lose even more, and the macro accentuates the fact that you are wrong. These are very difficult times, and a lot of people are giving up.

Randy: Yes. It's happening quite a bit.

K: How are you dealing with the emotionality of it?

R: I think it's a great opportunity. I made fourteen million dollars in February [2008], the most volatile month on the calendar in the past five years because this is the stuff that I have been waiting for. You know when you are trying to wait for a fast pitch, and you see a hundred of them come at a time; you hit them out of the park. It's been like spring training. The guy is throwing me fastballs, and I am ready for them. I don't understand why everyone is afraid of getting hit. We knew that there were going to be fastballs. Not everything is a softball.

This is exactly how people lose a lot of money. I mean, it's human nature. They want to wait until it feels okay. You have to be willing to be uncomfortable and go after the opportunity when no one else is willing to do so.

K: You have to be willing to play when you're uncomfortable.

R: I believe that fear influences the market value for every stock. When it's dislocated, by definition that's the opportunity, because there are more sellers than buyers. If it's like this every day, where is the big opportunity?

K: Are you handling the emotion better now than you did in the past? What have you learned about yourself and emotions in recent years?

R: I think it's a battle every time you step onto the field. I go through my steps of what's going to make me feel more confident, but it's not stopping me from being nervous about what's going on. Then I start doing the work, and then through the work, the emotion comes down. Then I kind of recognize that it's just a feeling and that I can make the feeling go away. What I find is that inaction creates that feeling and doesn't make it go away.

K: What's the feeling?

R: Anxiety. It requires work, but I've been there before, and I know that if I just practice it ahead of time, I will feel confident when it comes. We are not going to be surprised.

K: So preparation reduces the anxiety?

R: Completely.

K: What have you learned that you didn't know before?

R: I learned that you have to believe in the game and believe that all of this isn't for nothing. You have to believe that you are not fooling yourself. You have to believe the result and the work.

K: Are you doing more work now than you did in the past?

R: No. I have just gotten better at it. I am proactive as opposed to reactive.

K: Are there more things to be prepared for?

R: I just learned a new one today. I asked a guy, "How do you back into the international number?" Then he showed me on a website. I always wondered how people got that number. Now I just tested that three times today. You can always improve your game.

K: So, as you have improved your game, what has happened?

R: The anxiety comes off. Repetition also plays a part. What I am trying to do is to alleviate my anxiety. I have gone through the other quarters; so I am not going to feel anything other than the work when the time comes. I think about it a lot. I was watching the Masters, and this guy is teeing off, and he has a gallery full of spectators. I mean they can't be more than ten feet away from him when he tees off, but he is focused on the target. The way he must be able to do that is that he doesn't see the people, and he has done this so many times before.

K: The best pitchers don't even see the batter. They see the strike zone. They see the catcher's mitt. They know how to release the ball and are aggressive. They don't care if they are getting close to the batter. They are dominating the batter, and they know it. They are not doing it to fool the batter. If they are focused, then the batter is irrelevant. In effect, trading mastery results from developing objectivity about your trading and the ability to detach yourself from the emotional response to the markets and your performance so that you can be as focused and disciplined as possible.

The key to continuing to succeed even in the midst of uncomfortable feelings is to recognize that emotions are not reality. They are simply feelings about a situation, and we ought not to confuse our feelings about reality with reality itself.

For example, a trader who cannot master his fears will worry about how he is doing and how he looks. This concern inevitably affects his interpretation of events. In other words, he buys a stock, and the stock goes down. He begins to wonder why the stock is going down, but he keeps holding. In fact, thinking it will go up any minute, he adds to it. As the stock continues to go down, and he continues to lose more money, he begins to get panicky. He finally gets out after losing six points instead of losing one.

His emotions interfered with his trading, because first he was in denial of the actual events as they were taking place, and then he panicked as he realized the losses he was going to incur. He allowed his emotional responses to dictate his reaction rather than calling around to get more information and finding the reason for the drop.

Excessive emotional involvement can even build into paranoia, where we are reacting more to our feelings than to reality itself. The more we rely on our emotions, the more confused we become and the more we experience anxiety. So, how can you learn to live with the uncomfortable feelings that come as a result of reality without allowing those feelings to color the way in which you trade?

First, recognize the problem so that you don't perpetuate it. Failure to identify the issues leads to a lot of scurrying about, noise, and random searching behavior, but no problem solving. Recognizing the problem reduces the suffering. It may not eliminate the problem, but it reduces the distress.

Next, own the problem. Don't try to rationalize or justify your actions. Simply admit the facts. This is what happened. This is what I did. Once you are able to look objectively at a situation, you will be able to move forward at a much faster and more successful pace. When you are too busy trying to defend yourself, you are not open to instruction from the past or from peers. You are resistant and fighting things over which you have no control. This serves only to stifle growth and cause frustration.

Then, make a conscious decision not to act impulsively or automatically in an effort to eliminate feelings of discomfort or negative thoughts. Notice the feelings. Notice the thoughts. Recognize that they are not pleasant but move forward with determination and a clear presence of mind, reacting to the events at hand—not to the feelings you have conjured up as a result of the events. You shouldn't waste time trying to change your thoughts or how you feel. Just notice them. Notice how long they last and how they color your trading experiences. Notice the constant conversation or chatter of your mind, all the thoughts you have about who you are, the meaning of things, what others mean, and your interpretations of the markets. Just notice them, and let them pass, learning to stay centered in the present moment.

Keep coming back to the present moment. Keep coming back to your plan of action, what you know, not what you feel, away from the off-kilter thoughts which impel you to become distracted by negative impulses.

Teaching Traders Self-Assessment and Self-Control

Not every trader instinctively knows how to monitor his emotions. In fact, you may find this ability to be one of the hardest to discover among potential candidates. Fortunately, it is one that can be taught. Try teaching your traders to do the following:

- Encourage them to keep a log of their trades. A log enables them to examine what exactly took place in a given trade and how they responded to it. For example, say they bought a stock at 20. They planned to do a little more work to take a larger position, but it started to move against them. By logging their emotions as well as the physical manifestations of the trade, they can review exactly what they were experiencing.
- Have them review their log, considering how they were feeling and how those feelings affected their actions and reactions in the trade. Did they get out at the appropriate time? Did they hang on in false hope? Was their decision an emotional one, or was it based on data?
- Ask them to make an effort to become more aware of their emotional responses and how their emotions influence their trading. As they become conscious of their emotional reactivity, they will be more likely to observe the repetitiveness of their actions and not act impulsively.

MANAGING STRESS WELL

I recently talked to one successful manager about how he was handling the continuing decline in the retail space in which he traded. Perry was typical of what I would consider a successful manager who had no shame in admitting that he was disappointed with his performance and 50 percent decline in overall P&L since the peak of his year in early June. He admitted that the mixture of the subprime mortgage decline, credit crunch, high oil prices, and bad weather had hurt retail sales and that he was basically treading water and trying to risk-manage his positions to keep his losses contained, waiting for the time when fundamentals would once again matter in the marketplace, thus preserving some firepower so he could get bigger in his high-conviction ideas. What I liked hearing was his candor in describing his stress and the fact that he had a methodology for containing risk, paring down his book and waiting patiently for the markets to recover. Perry illustrates what I would call *mastery*, the capacity to function fully in the world with the resources available to you.

If you were able to talk to your money managers, what would you want to ask them about their state of mind and their strategies for dealing with market downturns and portfolio drawdowns? In the following, I outline a number of things to look for when evaluating the performance of portfolio mangers and trying to coach them through difficult periods when they may be distracted by stress and veering from their proven strategies. When talking to your fund managers, realize that some might not appreciate being questioned in such a laser-like way. However, the real players will welcome the opportunity to share their experiences and to reflect on how well they are playing their "A" game. Consider:

- Does he have a rational explanation for fluctuations in his performance during times of market stress and volatility?
- Is he clear about the explanations for any bad results without rationalizing his performance by comparing himself to others or blaming the markets or other circumstances?
- Does he seem irritable, unavailable, and frustrated?
- Does he answer your questions without being evasive or exaggerating his level of confidence?

The best managers are intellectually honest, respect the fragility/volatility of the markets, and have had sufficient experience with market reversals that they have learned and demonstrated an ability to recover from adversity. They also have prepared for a variety of doomsday scenarios, handle unraveling markets with aplomb, and can explain complex concepts in plain English:

- Does he have a research process?
- Has he or his team visited the company and its competitors, and talked to suppliers, vendors, and customers so that they really understand the drivers of the company's profitability cycle, or are they simply looking at companies from a top-down or macroeconomic perspective and betting on a theme?
- What is the quality of the data he is assessing?
- If he is involved in consumer-related stocks, is he looking at consumer spending data, consumer income data, and mortgage reset data?
- Does he have a handle on mortgage delinquency rates?

- Does he have some measured opinions about the Fed easing of the discount rate to produce liquidity without overstimulating consumer spending and causing inflation?
- What is his proactive strategy for making money?

While you don't have to know all the specifics about this kind of analytical data, you do want reassurance that these kinds of issues are being examined. During difficult times, the best PMs pare down their portfolios, eliminate ideas with a low probability of producing profits, and concentrate on building up their highest-conviction ideas with a 50 percent upside probability and possessing a differentiated view from street consensus, a confident fundamental story, and the likelihood of upcoming catalysts. While goal-oriented with a portfolio of high-conviction ideas and the anticipation of specific price movement over selected time horizons, they are also comfortable staying with their ideas during periods of market volatility. Ask yourself:

- Does he have a well-defined risk management process?
- Are his best ideas in the portfolio and sized correctly (e.g., putting 5 to 10 percent of his capital in his highest-conviction ideas)?
- Has he hedged the portfolio with specific short ideas that provide protection against market volatility and the potential for generating profits in their own right?
- Does the fund keep a comprehensive set of risk metrics so as to be able to demonstrate a greater number of winning versus losing trades (55 to 60 percent being good) and a positive slugging ratio or W/L ratio where they are making more money in their winning trades than in their losing trades?
- Are they running with a Sharpe risk-adjusted return ratio of 1.5 or better?
- Is he reducing his overall use of capital in times of market volatility or drawdowns so that he has firepower left to get bigger in his high-conviction ideas when the drawdown ceases and the recovery period starts?
- Does he have a strategy to take down exposure consistent with a bearish perspective, or is he building up at such times, trying to maintain the same levels of profitability as he did when things were bullish?

Too often, inexperienced managers use all of their capital, lose big when the markets go down, and have little in reserve to take advantage of the market reversals.

- Does he have a thorough process in place to ensure that he is hiring the right kinds of analysts or PMs to work in his hedge funds?
- How thorough and sound are his hiring practices?
- Are incentives properly aligned with the goals of the firm?
- Are the best practices in place to ensure retention of top talent over the long haul?
- What is the quality of the money being invested in this fund?
- Is it short-term money with easy redemption terms such that during any downturn there are going to be redemptions?

Additionally, it is useful to consider whether the manager is willing to tell you about his strategy.

- Does he have a balanced portfolio?
- Is he fully invested and adequately hedged?
- How is the portfolio doing relative to the overall markets in his sector?
- Is he up when the rest of the market is down?
- Is he regularly reviewing his portfolio to see what is working, what isn't working, and what more he needs to do to tweak his strategy?
- Did the catalysts or events that he factored into his analysis come about? Catalysts can include reports on earnings results, guidance, and quality of margins.
- Were there any government announcements that might have a positive effect on specific stocks? Has the sell-side (the brokers and banks) given any hint about upcoming events that might impact his holdings?
- Is the PM making money in both his core longs and core short positions, suggesting he has a plan and is executing a good hedging strategy?

Developing the trader's edge requires staying calm and managing risk in periods of great market volatility. The toughest lesson for most PMs is to cut losses and to get out of trades that aren't working, especially during periods of drawdowns. At such times, it is critical to deal with the stress and psychology of drawdowns and the importance of cutting losses.

"These periods tend to follow euphoric periods when it's just too easy, when everyone is making money," explained Matt, a manager who successfully navigated the difficult markets of 2007–2008.

You feel like you are brilliant. That's a precursor; you are usually within weeks at that point. So we try to look for when we are being sloppy. It's all indicative of being willing to move out on that risk curve. If we are doing it, other people are doing it, which means the whole system thinks it's smart. You feel like you are smart when you have made a lot of money. When you start to see that people are doing really well, that it's really easy, then I think you should take your gross down in advance. I firmly believe that people make irrational decisions with respect to what they are in.

The best managers recognize stress and separate out their own emotional responses from their behavior as a PM. They also have an inordinate desire to win and are continually tracking for what can go wrong. This, coupled with their objectivity, enables them to quickly identify when something has changed and motivates them to react in a proactive way. They recognize that bad streaks happen, and they are prepared to adapt. They have a process but don't stubbornly stick to past strategies and are able to adapt to changing circumstances.

It is not that the best performers don't experience stress; it is that they have a process that insulates them from their own stress response and enables them to continue to invest in a rational and profitable way. A critical aspect of this process is to master stress not only in terms of portfolio management processes but also by building teamwork and leadership skills, something that I will discuss in more detail in the next chapter.

 CHAPTER IN REVIEW

1. The key to trading success is to promise or commit to a stretch target over a specified time horizon and then construct a strategy to reach this target. As easy as this may sound, it is not particularly easy to implement, especially in turbulent times when traders are feeling very stressed and pulled out of their game.

2. Your capacity to cope effectively is significantly reduced by the overreaction of your nervous system. If you don't recognize what is happening and attempt to deal with your stress responses, you are likely to become overwhelmed.

3. Therefore, to manage anxiety and fear while dealing with the uncertainty of the market, you must become comfortable with uncomfortable feelings. You have to notice and separate your emotional responses from the decisions that you are making.

4. When a trader reacts to his emotions, he often tricks himself into believing false notions about himself and his abilities—either overvaluing his abilities or undervaluing his potential. A trader who is able to observe his own emotions, without reacting to them, has to have both self-discipline and good self-esteem.

5. An individual with good self-esteem will rebound from failure, often seeing a missed shot or a blown trade simply as a challenge to win at the next opportunity. In order to be willing to risk—in order to be willing to be wrong on occasion, to make a mistake, to look badly—an individual's self-esteem must be sufficient to allow this.

6. The ability to self-assess after periods of drawdown demonstrates great self-awareness, lack of defensiveness, and willingness to change and to listen to coaching recommendations—all signs of someone with the capacity to adapt and win.

7. The less skilled or experienced manager doesn't have a process, holds onto his losers, chases flyers, overreacts to the market drawdown or gets paralyzed, rationalizes his performance, justifies, gets irritated, and is avoidant. He lacks discipline, gets emotionally attached to positions, and forms conclusions based on faulty notions.

8. Attachment to ideas based on how we feel is a primary source of confusion, because our feelings are always subject to contradiction and doubt. Stress comes from the emotional overlay on top of the experience.

9. The key to continuing to succeed even in the midst of uncomfortable feelings is to recognize that emotions are not reality. You can do that by recognizing the problem so that you don't perpetuate it, owning the problem, and then making a conscious decision not to act impulsively or automatically in an effort to eliminate feelings of discomfort or negative thoughts.

10. Developing the trader's edge requires staying calm and managing risk in periods of great market volatility—cutting losses and getting out of trades that aren't working, especially during periods of drawdowns. At such times, it is critical to deal with the stress and psychology of drawdowns and the importance of cutting losses.

CHAPTER 6

Nurturing Team Players

Listening, Learning, and Working Together

For college basketball fans, the run to the Sweet 16 during March Madness of 2008 brought an exciting finish and excellent example of teamwork for one up-and-coming, relatively unknown team seeking to make a mark in basketball history.

After a dramatic comeback that led to overtime play, Western Kentucky University was moments away from ending their season. The Toppers were down by 1 with little more than 5 seconds left in play when Tyrone Brazelton got the ball and made a mad dash down the court. Brazelton was having a career-high game, having already scored 33 points including six 3-pointers. He was hot and, all things considered, relatively open for the shot. But then he made a surprising and likely legendary move. Brazelton passed the ball backward to teammate Ty Rogers, a senior guard, who then made the game-winning, last-second, never-forget-me, 3-point basket that will inevitably go down in NCAA history. Instantaneously, Ty Rogers became famous. His shot was literally plastered on newspapers and Internet sites and replayed hundreds of times on radio and TV broadcasts for days and weeks afterward.

Rogers got his piece of college basketball fame, but what about Brazelton? Why did he do it? Given the percentages, the likelihood of his hitting the shot was just as great, if not much greater than passing it off to Rogers. He could have shot it. He might have made it. Why did he give away his big chance at fame? As he said, "It wasn't about scoring. It was

143

about winning" (*The Daily News*, Saturday, March 22, 2008, p. 3B). That is the attitude of a team player.

While some erroneously consider trading an individual endeavor, in fact, the most successful traders are very much team players. Team players understand that working together not only can contribute to the success of the fund, but can also enhance one's individual success as well. Therefore, a team player has a strong motivation to make the players around him better and is willing to sacrifice his momentary achievement for the overall team good.

CHARACTERISTICS OF A TEAM PLAYER

A team player is cooperative, interested in helping others, and able to subdue his own ego for the good of the organization. He is not overly introspective or selfish. He understands the value of sharing and places greater importance on the good of the group and the benefit of others than on his own selfish interests. He recognizes the impact he can have on others by exemplifying an accepting and encouraging attitude. He looks for ways to communicate his needs with teammates and finds similar ways in which he can support them in their efforts. He is honest but respectful of the sensitivities of others and looks for ways of communicating in a supportive, nonthreatening, nonnegative way. He is able to encourage his teammates to persevere during defeat, and is confident enough to help push them to move beyond their comfort zones.

A team player makes a conscious effort to abide by shared team values and those things that represent good character. He recognizes that his thoughts and actions impact not only his own behavior but also the behavior, responses, and contributions of those on his team. Therefore, he functions in a committed way; he is committed to his objectives as well as to the good of the team and to adhering to a sound set of moral values.

While some people seem to be born team players, it isn't a skill that has to be inborn. Successful businesses all over the world have learned the value of instilling a team philosophy among their employees. Traders are no different. What isn't inherited can be taught.

Responsible

A team player takes charge of his actions and takes responsibility for how he is performing. He doesn't allow too much emotion or irrationality to intrude on his processes and has developed his capacity for concentration on the critical elements of the tasks. He visualizes the steps he will take before he engages proactively in preparation and trading and has an observing ego for monitoring his concentration so that he can tune out distracting thoughts and bring more intensity to the processes at hand. He continually works to improve his performance and to tune out anxiety and extraneous signals and the reactions of others so that he is totally focused on the task at hand. He is able to control his own inclination to please others and therefore to modify his behavior. This means learning to tune out fearful and negative thoughts and the negative opinions of others who themselves are overcautious naysayers, and to tune into only those who support his desire to achieve successful outcomes.

A team player recognizes that he alone is in control of his actions and that ultimately he must focus more on his own behaviors than on his results. Of course, the results might provide a clue as to whether he was focused and committed and might provide the framework for the actions he must take, but he doesn't judge himself by his results or by the opinions of others, only by the degree to which he is involved in his processes and is continually improving what he can do. He doesn't attribute his successes or failures to others, to the market, or to factors over which he has no control. He is very objective about recognizing when he is engaged and what more he needs to do to be fully engaged in his processes.

Given this, the team player is also able to correct for his own past errors or mistakes in attitude and recognizes that he has a choice as to how he is going to function and doesn't have to stubbornly hold onto old habits simply because he has done so in the past. He is continually self-correcting and improving his ability to contribute to the larger effort of the group and is able to recognize when he has held back, had a negative attitude, or been reactive because of his own automatic responses to anxiety, threats, symbolic dangers, or some unconscious psychological need to have things his own way.

Positive and Encouraging

A team player sees the glass as half full. He has a positive outlook when faced with problems and focuses on the processes to improve performance. He doesn't get hung up on worrying about the outcome but focuses on the steps necessary to achieve the objective and gets satisfaction from doing the job well. He sees adversity as a challenge rather than as a source of failure and is not inclined to pity himself but is able to rise to the occasion and take on the challenge proactively.

The value of a little bit of encouragement goes a long way and can accomplish many positive responses from the members of the team. Therefore, it is important to encourage teammates and to find the buttons that motivate them. For example, one team leader discovered that a little note can make a big difference. After receiving a positive note about his write-ups, Sean began following the advice given to him at a previous meeting, which was to concentrate on his game and learn what works for him. He began figuring out that he needs to know the stocks, have a feel for relevant events that will move the needle, and know when to size up, hedge correctly, and the like. One little note of encouragement made a world of difference.

A manager named Peter seeks to build up his team by empowering people and aligning their interests with the goals of the firm. He is supportive as he delegates functions to people and is starting to see the fruits of his efforts as the traders on his team are becoming more involved in the recruiting of talent. He is also making an effort to train people to do the kinds of presentations that he is looking for and takes time to make sure they are making crisp and well-thought-out presentations before they present.

One way to build a supportive team is by arranging a time for traders to share. At a specified meeting, have the team share specific yearly goals and the strategies they intend to follow to reach them. An additional component may be to get them to talk briefly about what habits they need to be aware of to ensure that they reach their goals, as well as what they have learned in the past year that they are going to try to correct or modify. Of course, you should lead by example; therefore it would be very powerful for you to share some of your own objectives and strategies for reaching them. What are you going to do differently this year? What is your read of the markets and the economy?

The best team players are those who recognize the power of their own thoughts and make an active effort to instill positive thoughts about their performance, visualize positive results, and shift their thinking whenever negative thoughts or old life principles of self-doubt and uncertainty intrude on their consciousness and begin to influence the way they perform. They are skilled at blocking out negative thoughts from their past or from the intrusions of others. Thus, they are also skillful in helping teammates bypass negative thoughts. They listen to their teammates and encourage them to look at things from a broader perspective, all the time hearing their

teammates and not ridiculing them or minimizing the impact of their negative thoughts.

Sometimes traders don't realize how much of a negative attitude they
are carrying around and how their negativity affects those around them.
For example, Dale seemed oblivious to the fact that he was considered
confrontational and dismissive. He did not realize that he had a negative
image among potential candidates to the firm as well as from people around
the firm and elsewhere. When approached, he was somewhat incredulous
and had very little awareness of the impact he was having on others.

To his credit, he accepted the negative characterization and in fact became very open, receptive, and eager to learn what he was doing wrong
and how he could correct it. This led to questioning him about his style of
work and how he relates to others, and to an interesting review of his life
experience, which included the fact that he started working at age 14 and
worked his way through college without parental support and became very
self-sufficient at an early age. We explored the possibility that his style of
self-sufficiency and avoidance of others may be creating some of the reaction that the firm is hearing about.

Dale admitted that in the past he had been very aggressive with companies and that he has matured and no longer does that. He also admitted that
he has nothing to do with certain sell-side analysts with whom he used to
interact since he no longer thinks they provide value to him. He recognized
that perhaps this may not be endearing him to the Street.

He is quite aware that he consciously avoids people at the firm and in
the marketplace who have (in his mind) little to offer him. I inferred that
perhaps his self-sufficiency and critical nature (more of himself, but also
of others) may be conveying an arrogance and stirring resentment among
others, which has resulted in his present image problem. He took to heart
a lot of what was discussed and stated that he was willing to make some
efforts to start interacting in a more positive way with people. We talked
about the importance of working on himself and humanizing his relationships with people at the firm.

A positive attitude toward helping the team includes an ability to focus on doing what is required to get the job done, focusing on process,
focusing on the steps to succeed, and a relentless pursuit of doing the right
thing and not focusing on one's own feelings, the views of others, and the
concern with image. If an individual is like Dale and has a negative attitude, or is pessimistic or self-critical, or is constantly berating himself and
sees no possibility of improvement or success he will create a self-fulfilling

prophecy for himself as well as having a negative effect on others. If he is too concerned with his image, he may focus on creating an illusion about himself and try to manage the expectations and the comments others may make about him. He will then be busier managing his image than focusing on what it is that can enhance his performance in terms of doing what is best for the team. Such individuals may sometimes look so good that they succeed temporarily, but eventually, because much of their success is based on creating illusions about themselves, they are likely to fall dramatically when their efforts to cover up their weaknesses, indecisiveness, or self-interest become apparent to others.

It is therefore important to be careful in recruiting people to weed out those who are so perfectionist, self-critical, skeptical, paranoid, and helpless that their attitude will inflict damage on the morale of the group as well as on their own performance. This is not to say that you are looking for people with a Pollyanna attitude, who can see no wrong in anything. You are looking for objective realists who can face up to bad news, roll with the punches, and continually adapt to the changing requirements of the job and the marketplace.

Here you are looking for people who are resilient, flexible, adaptable, and willing to keep working on themselves so as to increase their ability to contribute to the efforts of the team. This means you want people who have the capacity to choose to act differently and to learn and adapt and who don't have to keep beating themselves or holding onto negative views.

Competitive

The team player is competitive and seeks to focus on the necessary processes to produce outstanding results. He is mentally tough, overcoming fear and anxiety and excessive preoccupation with the results and the opinions of others, and keeps doing the best he can by focusing on the tasks at hand. He is adaptable and seeks to find the most appropriate behavior for different situations, but, despite his willingness to help encourage and motivate his teammates, he will rarely if ever bend over backward to accommodate others just to promote a "nice" self-image. That doesn't mean that he isn't a nice person, but in the context of performance he is task and process oriented, and interested in delivering the results, not in winning a popularity contest.

As a competitor, he stays focused throughout the duration of a trade or investment and is careful not to become complacent, to let up or become overconfident too soon before the result is achieved. He recognizes that consciousness of purpose must be maintained until the results are finally in.

For example, Owen is a competitive trader who wants to be at the top of the leader board, but he is still willing to mentor a fellow trader and to share his best practices with others. Interestingly, he is willing to do this by way of improving his own game and because he is confident enough about himself to do this. Someone who is too competitive and simply wants to beat others may be less willing to share unless the culture puts a value on sharing and acknowledges his efforts to do so.

Coachable

An important aspect of cooperativeness is the individual's coachability and receptivity to changing attitudes, learning best practices and finding ways of improving his individual contribution to the team effort. A lot of people have a lot of intellect, drive, skill, and ambition but are self-centered. They like autonomy and are sometimes unreceptive to coaching or to suggestions on how to enhance their performance. The ability to be coached is especially important in team activities and in encouraging collaborative efforts; this sometimes takes a greater degree of humility, self-awareness, and willingness to change.

In my opinion, coachability is a critical variable. When you have a group meeting and are trying to help people learn new behaviors, you want team members who are receptive to learning what more they can do, and are willing to face their own resistance and get past what has been called *positionality*, where they are reluctant to move past the positions they hold in order to take on new functions and a new attitude that will enhance the group. Too much resistance or self-absorption can have a negative impact on others and discourage group participation and involvement in activities for the greater good.

Unfortunately, not all traders are coachable. Casey is a PM candidate who was well received by most PMs who evaluated his ideas. However, after further consideration, we found that he might not be too coachable.

Though Casey is a solid, cautious, and thorough risk-taker, he is not accommodating or flexible in his approach with other people. He is very self-reliant and doesn't put much value on the opinions of others (which can sometimes be a good thing but indicates a low tolerance for coachability). He is not a very empathetic person and is reserved and serious in his demeanor. Casey is not a relationship-oriented person and has trouble looking beyond his own self-interests in order to coach others or receive coaching from others; therefore he has problems with collaborative-type projects.

This is an interesting issue. Some people, like Casey, seem to have an inordinate capacity and desire for autonomy—the need to work independently of others and without supervision. They are resistant to any kind of management or efforts to get them to participate in team activities. They are individual performers and may have been good singles tennis players but not particularly adept at team sports such as basketball. They prefer to be in environments where they can select their own tasks and procedures and where there is a high degree of reliance on their individual efforts rather than on their contribution to the team.

These people are often reluctant to accept coaching, especially as it pertains to working with others, helping others, or even getting help for themselves. They may be highly competitive and focus a lot of their energy in outdoing others rather than in looking for ways to collaborate. They may be better suited for "eat what you kill" environments rather than ones that focus on team building and sharing of best practices. They are most satisfied by tasks that enable them to achieve individual goals by direct competition with themselves or others. This drive for autonomy can be so great that they may have difficulty meeting the requirements outlined by a firm in regard to doing things in a particular way. They cannot get out of their own way long enough to see the bigger picture.

This doesn't mean that they can't perform. They just have a strong need to do it their own way. Sometimes this works, but if you are trying to build a team culture, these types of individuals may not be the best candidates. They are naturally averse to giving any priority to the needs and expectations of others so that they are rarely able to tune into the needs of their colleagues, let alone the organization. If they are forced to function in terms of the needs of others, they will most likely fail to meet expected standards or their commitments. This has a much lower order of priority for them, and this keeps them from being as valuable as teammates as they can be. They sometimes try to work around rules, which they see as impediments to getting things done. Going even further, they are unlikely to see that their own behavior may trigger nonresponsiveness and nonsupportiveness in others, thereby creating the self-fulfilling prophecy that they are actually best off relying on themselves. They dismiss teamwork issues as "just talk and politics," not as critical to the improvement of a functioning organization.

Coachability, therefore, requires humility and understanding that there is always more to learn about being focused and getting the process right. A coachable trader is able to review what went wrong and what is needed to improve. He understands his teammates who may be breast-beating and down on themselves and is able to help them get past this self-sabotaging technique and focus on specifics that they can control. He recognizes that learning new things and implementing them requires change and that change isn't always comfortable. Still, he focuses on ways of solving problems rather than focusing on the problems themselves and, as such, is open to the suggestions and observations of others. He recognizes that a coach has a little more objectivity and can help him overcome the natural inclination to slack off.

In short, team players are people with interpersonal skills who are not reluctant to admit that they don't know, and are willing to try new things and to innovate and experiment and find others in the firm who can support them. This kind of learning attitude creates a collaborative environment where people can create all kinds of opportunities for themselves and the firm.

FINDING COMPLEMENTS TO YOUR TEAM

Finding team players doesn't mean just looking for the "smart guys." You have to find people who will fit the culture of your team and who have the requisite personality characteristics already discussed. Individuals may be excellent candidates, but if they don't complement the existing skills or the management style of the team leader they are ultimately not going to fit very well.

Instead of trying to make a square peg fit into a round hole, look for the round pegs for the round holes and the square pegs for the square holes. Here you want to be looking for people who fit your team culture, and who have a capacity to relate to others, build and sustain relationships, and adapt to changes that are required.

For example, Donald is a very bright and intense but pleasant guy with a lot of experience in doing very deep, fundamental, company-specific research in the technology space, looking for the anchoring and embedded value in company product cycles that will produce a solid stream of discounted cash flow in the future. He has a very sophisticated methodology that enables him to find value in the realm of what he considers the margin of safety, which tends to get him an edge very early in the investment cycle. He started working as a writer in the technology field in 1983, fresh out of university, graduated to a role as a technology analyst, and eventually ran a technology book for a while and has been running his own fund for the past several years.

While quite flexible about what he would be willing to do, he has always dreamed of teaching others when he "hung up his cleats." He is looking for a place where he can leverage his ideas, because his greatest satisfaction seems to be in the thought process to generate an edge in his analyses. He is used to working with others, and personality-wise, he describes himself as a very intense guy who has been softened by four years of psychotherapy.

He is very credible and is more interested in the intellectual process than in having to be the guy who pulls the trigger. He is very engaging, and Street smart enough to work with the older guys, yet bright enough to interact well and be of some added value to the younger players. He is also an experienced money manager and brings that kind of credibility to the game.

The only major weakness I found was his willingness to forgo running a book. I don't know how much that is evidence of his not being a goal-directed, driven kind of guy with a specific agenda, and how much it reflects his recognition that the game is getting too tough and he is willing to opt out to be part of a larger organization. From another angle, that may be a sign of maturity and self-awareness.

Given what was learned about Donald throughout the interview process, I suggested that he might be worth looking at as a potential Director of Research. He is extremely bright, has a good process, and would be good at managing a group of junior analysts as well as senior guys.

Remember, when seeking out team players it is just as important to recognize what you do *not* want. It's of interest that some people are so autonomous that they have little need for the support or acknowledgment of others. They are loners and are often viewed as not being good teammates. These people are often very stubborn and not very receptive to compromise or recognizing that it sometimes makes sense to give a little in order to gain a lot in the long run. Compromise often results in a win-win result and improves the quality of relationships and strengthens the interaction of a team. If someone seems hardwired against this kind of interaction but has an attitude of humility, a willingness to change, and a recognition of the value of working with others, then there is hope that he can become a team player.

CASE STUDY ON A COMPARISON OF TRADERS

An example of a good candidate who exemplifies a team player is Cory, a candidate for an analytical/quant team. Cory is a math undergrad with several years of experience doing event-driven strategies. He thinks probabilistically and has special skill at knocking out the noise, gaining clarity in crowded events, and considering binomial and trinomial solutions. He is particularly interested in series and sequences and numerical error approximation and combines mathematical modeling with creative thinking to calculate different event outcomes and timing.

Upon interviewing Cory, I found him to be very receptive, open to challenge and learning, and very self-examining and willing to adapt. He prefers a team environment to working in individual silos. He likes the philosophy of the organization and is very enthusiastic about being part of the team. Whereas he is very open, honest, and forthright, he likes debate and so may come off as a bit rough and prickly; however, he is quite receptive and very eager to get guidance from others so that he can improve.

His default style when stressed or challenged is to become more intense, quiet, and focused on the task at hand. His greatest strength (which he admits may at times be a weakness) is his tendency to be overanalytical and to dig deep for the meaning of things. He is very good at reading people and situations and analytical materials and very confident about what he knows. He believes that he could add immeasurably to the assessment of merger and acquisition materials based on his risk arbitrage experience. He is also inclined to be very competitive, especially with himself, and is very goal-oriented and focused on achieving results.

Cory is open, self-reflective, authentic, and of good character. Perhaps one of the most telling attributes was demonstrated by his concern for the company that he was leaving. He wanted to make sure that he helped them get set up for his transitioning out, which suggested to me that he had genuine concern for others over and above his own personal self-interest—the sign of a true team player.

On the other hand, Daniel is a trader who is seeking autonomy, freedom, recognition, and appreciation. He believes that he has earned the right to pick and choose his #2 and believes that he ought to be given the latitude to make such a choice, even though he is not inclined to present the idea in a forceful fashion. He is also of two minds about the processes and procedures in place. While he says that he is willing to cooperate with the due diligence and other processes in place, he quite clearly rankles at the idea that there is any oversight over his choices.

A lot of this is consistent with his personality profile of being a thinker and an innovator who would rather do things in his own way. He believes that he has enough experience in decision making and management of others to be able to do so. While Daniel frequently seeks advice about making decisions, this doesn't lend itself to team play or mentoring since he is self-obsessed and has trouble pulling the trigger, which may in fact reflect his basic problems in dealing with feeling managed by others.

This kind of conflict is reflective of the natural tension between management, which is trying to create stable processes and procedures, and the individualistic styles of creative types who prefer to do things their own way. Some of this creativity is good and shouldn't be stifled. However, there needs to be some structure to provide stability and continuity for the firm. Balancing the two is the ultimate challenge of teamwork and leadership, and Daniel has trouble with this.

Take two more examples. Kevin is very self-assured, aggressive, and assertive and has a strong need or ego drive to dominate or persuade others to his point of view. He is quick to assume the role of teacher and mentor, even to his peers and contemporaries. This sometimes comes off as a bit overconfident and overpowering, but because of his high level of gregariousness and empathy he generally is well liked and able to engage people in a pleasant way without offending them. No one has complained to me about his overbearingness.

Kevin is very quick to respond to challenges and rejections and keeps a positive outlook on things. He is also quite eager to self-examine and consider what he needs to do to continue to persuade people to his point of view and has a lot of concern about whether people respond to him and like him.

This is to be contrasted with Marcus, who is the overall head of the group and who has little concern about what people think about him. He has no need to convince people of his viewpoint, and if they don't get what he wants, he is quick to dismiss them and not put any time into working with them to help them improve. He has a lot of people complaining about his condescending and dismissive manner, and I have heard a lot of complaints about his abrasive, take-no-prisoners attitude. He is aware of this, but is convinced that he gets results, and that if people can't play by his rules they ought to go elsewhere.

Ideally, you want teammates who have the capacity to listen and to learn how to respond appropriately. If they don't have a natural inclination to be empathetic, they should recognize that area of weakness and be willing to spend some time learning to listen to others and finding ways of being supportive to others. Unfortunately, this is often easier said than done. Even many empathic people are so busy trying to be supportive that they offer help without considering the needs and expectations of those upon whom they are bestowing their help.

Build your team upon people who are not quick to jump in with their own preconceived judgments but are able to listen to their teammates and pick up subtle body language cues and other communication signals so as to better support others and align their interests toward the common good. You want people who either have the skill of empathy or are willing to *learn* to listen to others and give them the chance to share their concerns and alternative views. You want people who are willing to accept ideas that differ from their own and are not so convinced about their own handle on things that they cannot grow by participating and interacting with others.

THE IMPORTANCE OF COMMUNICATION

Building a team is a matter of building relationships, and the key to doing this is communication. Good communication consists not only of the verbal guidance given to team members. It also considers the impact of the words you decide to use to motivate others, the correct timing of advice, criticism, and encouragement, and the proper mixture of support during the review process to ensure that there is always a positive message and that people are not turned off or too focused on the negative. It also includes body language and facial gestures and knowing when to stay quiet as well as when to speak.

While it may take time for people to change their basic, underlying approach to interpersonal relationships, there is value in getting everyone on the same page in terms of shared concepts, a common set of distinctions, and greater consciousness about opening up dialogues throughout the firm. As mentioned earlier, some of this takes a certain degree of patience in listening to others to try to understand not only what they are saying but also what they mean by what they say. It means trying to decipher what concerns they have and not jumping to conclusions solely based on your own limited experience.

But to successfully communicate you must also maintain the confidence of your team members and take into consideration how to best align their emotional interests with the goals of the organization. You have to be clear about requests and commitments and get definition on deliverables and timelines. You must make sure that what people hear is what you intended to communicate. To ensure that you are on the same page, it is useful to periodically check with your listener as to whether you heard their concerns correctly and whether they understand what your requests are. The more effort that goes into clarification of messages, the more quickly you and your team members can function on the same page with the same priorities. One practical exercise to help with this is to repeat what you have heard to make sure that you are actually processing what the other person said.

It is also important to review your messages, especially when people are responding to you with bafflement and incredulity. It is important to clarify when this is happening and to redefine what your objectives, processes, and strategies are for reaching your objectives so that everyone is aligned on the same targets. Too often there is a tendency to soft-pedal certain tough issues, giving the listener the sense that you don't really mean what you are saying. Put another way, people are not only listening to what you are saying, they are listening to the tone and inflection in your voice and whether there are telltale signs from your body and eye movements to suggest that you don't really mean what you are saying or are trying to whitewash an issue or slip something by them. Therefore, candor and honesty are ultimately essential to effective communication.

Where you are not in agreement with someone about what he is saying, it is important to convey that you *understand* what he is saying and where he is coming from even though you may draw different conclusions and interpretations from the same data set. This open-ended approach will give you greater ability to learn new things about how others think through situations, how they see the world, and how they have come to different conclusions based on a different thought process. This will expand your own insight into the way things work and will expand your ability to see the world from a number of different perspectives. In all of this, to be a good team member, you want to listen to others, *especially* to those with whom you don't agree, without judgment or criticism or any kind of attitude that will close off communication.

When faced with a difficult problem, brainstorm with others to identify resources for additional information. Collaborate with team members or members of management by bouncing ideas off of them. Recognize the contributions of colleagues and convey your appreciation of their value. The power of many can enhance a kernel of an idea.

Having a functional team requires that each individual learn how to deal with the complexity of having too many cooks in the kitchens. There is often tension between portfolio managers and investment professionals and the management side of the business. Subtle interactions require some savvy as well as a willingness to let go of ego or the desire to dominate others and make them wrong. Traders must recognize that certain processes are followed and that the intellectually driven side of the business doesn't dominate without regard for the need for controls and adherence to some larger policy issues. This is ultimately a creative process.

When traders have difficulty playing as a team, a number of different measures can be taken, but sometimes the easiest and most efficient is simply encouraging communication and offering mediation. For example, Keith and Wayne were having difficulties getting along. Keith was having problems with the allocation of P&L and felt that he wasn't getting sufficient credit and acknowledgment from Wayne for a successful trade. On the other end, Wayne felt that he was not receiving credit for his writeups. Therefore, feelings of injustice on both sides were causing these traders to be very preoccupied and frazzled.

A meeting was arranged where I served as the mediator. There were a lot of issues to discuss, most of which seemed to emanate from Keith, who felt he had added value to the trade from the time he said not to sell it at 86, that Wayne had done little value-added work since then, and that Wayne hadn't acknowledged Keith's contribution. Wayne for his part seemed very conciliatory and cooperative, apologetic, willing to acknowledge Keith, and the like.

The first suggestion was that when they are both involved in a trade and have differing views they need to sit down to discuss their differences and not let things build up. They agreed to negotiate whether to reallocate responsibility for the position at that time. They both agreed to a 50 percent split up to the present, and then a reallocation of a 20 percent (Wayne)/80 percent (Keith) split going forward.

While Wayne wasn't completely satisfied with the financial outcome, he said he would "take this one for the team." Keith was not completely satisfied, either, in that he still felt that he deserved more than the initial 50 percent. I discussed with Keith how this continual feeling of injustice seemed to be a longstanding life principle that was prohibiting him from being a productive leader and teammate. Both traders were encouraged to see the real value of the agreement as maintaining a good working relationship with each other for the future.

So, communication is the vehicle through which you can motivate your team members to realize their hidden potential and to perform way beyond their natural expectations. How you approach communication with your team members will have a significant impact on how they feel about you and the rest of the team, as well as the mutual efforts you are all making toward realizing a goal. Here it is critical to recognize that there are vast differences between barking orders to others and enrolling them in the process by trying to teach, educate, and nurture them toward mutually meaningful objectives; therefore, you should do your best to make your teammates feel appreciated and understood.

People want to be cared about, and it is important to determine the subtle needs and wants of the people on your team so that you can address their needs when presenting your vision and the values or behaviors you will expect from them and the kind of performance you will be evaluating. True teamwork involves not only focusing on the objectives of the organization but recognizing that the people in the organization are unique individuals with their own interests, sensitivities, and lives apart from the work situation. To the extent that you can relate to individuals as complete persons and recognize who they are, they will appreciate your interest and will feel that you have their best interests at heart and will then be better able to take your criticism and suggestions to improve performance.

Of course, as a good teammate you will be humble and recognize that you do not have all the answers, either, and that everyone can benefit mutually from the input of others. You should also be willing to find alternative views to solving problems. When everyone is contributing to the solution of a problem, there will be a larger frame of reference and a greater ability to move forward faster.

CHAPTER IN REVIEW

1. While some erroneously consider trading an individual endeavor, in fact the most successful traders are very much team players. Team players understand that working together can contribute to the success of the fund and can also enhance one's individual success.

2. A team player is cooperative, interested in helping others, and able to subdue his own ego for the good of the organization. He understands the value of sharing and places greater importance on the good of the group and the benefit of others than on his own selfish interests.

3. While some people seem to be born team players, it isn't a skill that has to be inborn. What isn't inherited can be taught.

4. A team player will be responsible, positive and encouraging, competitive, and coachable.

5. Individuals may be excellent candidates for a position, but if they don't complement the existing skills or the management style of the team leader, they are ultimately not going to fit very well. Instead of trying to make a square peg fit into a round hole, look for the round pegs for the round holes and the square pegs for the square holes.

6. The key to building good team relationships is communication. Good communication consists of verbal guidance, motivational words, the correct timing of advice, criticism, and encouragement, and the proper mixture of support. It also includes body language and facial gestures and knowing when to stay quiet as well as when to speak.

7. To successfully communicate, you must also maintain the confidence of your team members and take into consideration how to best align their emotional interests with the goals of the organization. You have to be clear about requests and commitments and get definition on deliverables and timelines. Make sure that what people hear is what you intended to communicate.

8. It is also important to review your messages, to clarify what is being said, and to redefine your objectives, processes, and strategies for reaching your objectives so that everyone is aligned on the same targets. Where you are not in agreement with someone about what he is saying, it is important to convey that you understand what he is saying and where he is coming from even though you may draw different conclusions and interpretations from the same data set.

9. Communication is the vehicle through which you can motivate your team members to realize their hidden potential and to perform way beyond their natural expectations. How you approach communication with your team

members will have a significant impact on how they feel about you and the rest of the team, as well as the mutual efforts you are all making toward realizing a goal.

10. True teamwork involves not only focusing on the objectives of the organization but recognizing that the people in the organization are unique individuals with their own interests, sensitivities, and lives apart from the work situation. To the extent that you can relate to individuals as complete persons and recognize who they are, they will appreciate your interest and will feel that you have their best interests at heart and will then be better able to take your criticism and suggestions to improve performance.

CHAPTER 7

Leadership

Directing Success

W ho can forget legendary coach Vince Lombardi? Known as one of the all-time greatest coaches in history, Lombardi was named "Coach of the Century" by ESPN, inducted into the Professional Football Hall of Fame, and had the Super Bowl trophy renamed in his honor. Under Lombardi's leadership, the Green Bay Packers collected six division titles, five NFL championships, and two Super Bowls. When his career ended, he had accumulated a record unmarred by a losing season, and the NFL named him the "1960s Man of the Decade."

What makes a coach like Lombardi such a successful leader? Is it an attitude, a work ethic, certain personality traits that he was born with, or skills that he learned? Is it a demand for attention or obedience, or a promise and delivery of success? As I have discussed throughout this book, I believe it is a combination of all these factors, as well as circumstances, which lead to an exemplary model of leadership like Lombardi.

Leadership is comprised of many variables, but all good leaders want to improve; they always want to win; they are committed to their objectives and willing to do what it takes to keep improving their performance and that of their team. Vince Lombardi said it best: "The spirit, the will to win and the will to excel are the things that endure. These qualities are so much more important than the events that occur."

EMPOWERING A CULTURE OF CHANGE

Leadership is ultimately about defining the vision of your team or organization and giving people the courage to create something that didn't exist before. Leadership involves more than mapping out a plan. It means defining the objective, developing a strategy, and empowering the members of your team to reach deeply into themselves to find the wherewithal to produce the results that you are seeking. It is a process that requires constant vigilance, support, and encouragement as well as firm timelines and a sense of accountability so that people are enrolled in the process and willing to take certain measured risks to embrace the unknown and commit to outstanding performance and outsized results. It involves the judicious use of the carrot and the stick, being assertive enough to lead others empathetically without bullying them, so that they don't lose their faith in your leadership.

Like Lombardi, the leader who is assertive is likely to communicate clearly to help his team members. He will be outspoken and willing to take the lead in encouraging his team. Given the right combination of empathy and aggressiveness he should be able to be forthright and strong at the same time as he tunes into the responses and reactions of those on his team. How well he leads will in large part depend on his willingness to adapt to the needs of those around him and to get past his own personal inclination, for example, to be concerned with such personal objectives as garnering the approval of others.

A good leader understands that others may have insights and abilities beyond the scope of his own knowledge and experience. As such, he will not rigidly cling to his opinions but will adjust to different perspectives. He will listen with intent to understand and identify opportunities and needs, rather than listening to formulate a response. He will encourage people to share their unique points of view and avoid the tendency to interrupt others before they finish explaining their point of view. He will try to understand where they are coming from rather than trying to point out why he thinks they're wrong or trying to persuade them to agree with him.

Case Study on Creating a Culture of Change

Randall is one of the premier hedge fund managers on Wall Street who, in a span of five years, has created one of the more successful multi-billion-dollar hedge funds. I spent time with him recently discussing some of his thoughts about leadership and how he has created a unique culture of collaboration at his firm with the hope that this would point to one way of empowering people.

Kiev: I wanted to pursue a few questions about leadership and culture, particularly culture. Can you talk about issues such as community, fairness, teamwork, and respect, because it seems to me that each firm has its own culture but few people really pay attention to it. It's almost like an after-thought.

Randall: Things like that are value statements. They have to be as relevant ten years from now and twenty years from now as they are today. Take a giant step back. What is it that makes us successful today that we also think can make us successful five years from now and ten years from now? What do we have to continue to do or reinforce or train beyond XYZ industry, XYZ stock, or XYZ strategy?

What makes certain teams great? What makes certain franchises great? Part of it is a system; there is an intelligent strategy, and we have an intelligent approach. It's an attitude, if you will. Sometimes they are explicitly stated, and sometimes they are just implicitly reflecting some captain or leader of the team, a strong presence or coach in the locker room.

K: Was this something you decided or was it a group effort? Could you expand on these values and how you introduced them to your firm?

R: I decided. We decided to start hiring some people in 2004. We were seventeen people, and we put out two business plans—one to get to thirty-five and one to get to fifty-five. The fifty-five was more of a three-year business plan.

K: How specific were you about the alignment of newcomers to the core values of the firm?

R: We want to tell them the basic patterns of what it means to be a part of our firm beyond "We are a hedge fund, and we are going to give you a job." We want to say "This is us" in very clear black-and-white language so that somebody else can read it and say, "Well, that's just not me," or "That is me."

K: Can you give me a specific example?

R: Teamwork is one of them. There are very good people in the money management business who said, "I want access to capital on a cost-efficient basis. I want to be aligned with a good series of individual performers so our collective performance will be good. I want to be aligned with the best marketing and distribution staff so they get the most resources. I need an individual who can just execute my business plan." I respect that, and that's a great person, and they could be great in money management, but I know they won't fit into this culture. So putting teamwork on there actually makes some sense, because somebody may look at it and say, "Look, that's an interesting value, and I understand the concept, but it's just not what I want out of my job."

K: What do you mean by *teamwork*?

R: I mean, literally, we will break down a name, and we will have an industry analyst cover from an industry perspective. If we are moving at different parts of the capital structure instead of buying the equity, if we are buying the bonds, our fixed income department will get involved. If we are not just doing the analytics but we are trying to get the anecdotes, our proprietary research team will get involved, and those guys will help do a bunch of channel checks. A bunch of senior guys will be looking at the name.

So, we are somewhat interchangeable; if one guy is busy, the other guy is there. If somebody is territorial, that just doesn't work. That type of open communication teamwork approach is a little bit harder to do. You're going to have to embrace it. You either have to want it or not. Some people don't. Some people say, "Look, I want all my process. I don't trust anybody else."

K: Have you had guys who said, "I really don't want to come here"?

R: Yeah. We respect that. We ask, "What is your goal in five years?" If they say, "I want to be a portfolio manager and running my own fund," that's fine, but that means that there is not going to be a long-term resource here, because we don't have that position open in five years. We can tell you that they're interested in getting the education, but they're not interested in being a long-term resource.

K: Having decided on the values, have you been able to implement those values in the culture such that the firm reflects them?

R: I think so. We do a good job of making sure that we are performing for the customers. I think that we truly feel that performance, personalize it, internalize it, and take it home with us, particularly at the senior level. We are literally ill if it's not working.

I think we have gotten it right, but that's a challenge over time. It's easier to get a meritocracy right if everybody starts at the same place and the same time. The gun goes off, and the faster runners get to the finish line faster. That's easy. What's harder is some guy has been here five or six years, and some of the other guys have been here for two years. On their merits, three guys may have had a much better year. How do you balance long term versus short term? Somebody was able to make it up the ladder and in eleven months get the promotion last time. We are a bigger organization. Does it now take eighteen months? Are we therefore slowing down? Those types of things are harder. We are a different business than we were three or four years ago. We don't want to kill that ability for somebody to come in and wow us and be a superstar. We want to have a superstar culture. I think the answer is that we are living our values that are written on that page. Some of them you need to continuously work at.

Fairness is one, and objectivity. It becomes really hard. You have to respect that the process was fair. If we are going to exist in a team process and a team investment approach, which is going to be based on facts and objectivity and rigorous analysis, we are all going to be open to somebody else's thoughts and comments. People have to trust the process by which we say "yes" to one idea and "no" to another idea. "Yes, we are going to pay this guy a lot of money," and "No, we're not going to pay this guy a lot of money." They have to trust that there is fairness in that process and it's not just, "That person is Randall's favorite, and he plays golf with him on the weekends," or something like that. It means consistency in the way we approach promotions and opportunity.

K: What about community?

R: Community is our eleventh value. I added community because if we're successful at the first ten we are going to create a lot of wildly successful professionals. What do I want to have happen? Do I want to have a bunch of guys driving Ferraris and belonging to the best golf club memberships and vacationing in the best islands and that's it? If we are successful, I would like to think that we did more than just make some spoiled brats rich. I would like to think we try to do something good with it. Bear Sterns was famous; four percent of your paycheck went to charity, and they audited your tax returns to prove it. We are not into that much of a mandate, but more by example and by including it as one of the core tenets.

Ultimately, a lot of our clients not only are going to judge us as performers, but they're going to judge us as people. You cannot look at the incentive comp system and the revenues of the hedge fund world and not understand that it takes a lot of hard work and effort. At the end of the day, even then everybody involved in this industry has to consider himself lucky. If we don't carry ourselves, not only myself as an individual, but if we don't carry ourselves as a firm in a way that represents well and give some of that back, then I think ego gets the best of us. I think we can kill the business that way, despite our performance. I thought it was important enough of an issue that it should be there firm-wide. Just last Friday we had our Philanthropy Day, where we encourage people to give time or give money or board representation or something. We want a hundred percent participation in something. We don't want to mandate what people's causes are. I don't really want to tie all of our giving together. I don't want to tell people whether they have to do time or have to do money. I do think that it would be great if everybody did something.

K: Do you get pretty good cooperation from that?

R: I would say that the wheels are turning, and they're picking up motion. In any group there are some people who naturally gravitate to it at all levels. There are some people who are the walk-a-thon people and the cause people at all levels. Some people have a specific aversion to it. I think the people on the fence are moving to become more active and more pronounced. That is, I think, the benefit of putting it out there.

K: Do you have any specific leadership strategies in terms of thinking about how to grow the business and how to build the culture, or is it enough that you have these values and you're conscious of them and remind people of them and select people in terms of them? Is there an ongoing effort to work on the culture?

R: Yes, we review people every six months. We are now broken down into seven different business functions and the research team. The research team is broken down into literally eleven different pods, some of which have management directors that run them and some of which are pods that float out there and become partners overseas. The values do come into the reviews. You know integrity doesn't really come into the reviews. If you don't have integrity in terms of the way you are doing your business, I bet you didn't make it to the review.

K: Have there been any changes in the organization over time, in terms of how you think?

R: Obviously, six years ago we functioned like a garage band, and three years ago a small band of leaders doing a lot of stuff. Today I would say the change is that I don't even oversee the overseers. That's where I think scaling your culture becomes important, because I can't literally sit down and micromanage and train for everything. It's like the constitution. These are the things that are unallowable. These are the things that everybody should look at and say, "All right, in this situation, what does this tell me to do?," and hopefully, if they have embraced these, then it's even better than my having to sit down and say, "Look, that's not really the right way to approach this."

K: Do you get a sense that other firms have this type of consciousness about these issues?

R: When Eton Park was formed, they sat down and watched the movie *Miracle*, a hockey movie about teamwork and stuff like that. It reinforces the fact that we are not alone and understanding that trying to build the fiber in essence to the firm is as important as populating the portfolio with good ideas.

K: How widespread is that?

R: I think it's a growing minority. There are not many majorities of firms out there doing it. My guess is if you don't have a culture that ties everybody together, that can be real damaging to a business longer term.

K: What about running into the resistance?

R: Running into resistance on how we should run the firm?

K: Yeah.

R: Part of it is capturing the high ground. To a certain extent, the troops all march to the same drumbeat if we agreed early on in the journey where we were all going. It helps to have had that clear vision. Of course, there are differences as to whether we staff more people, withdraw from an activity, and how do we do that. Again, that goes back to objectivity and fairness. We debate it just like we debate a stock. Ultimately, we are halfway between a partnership and a benevolent dictatorship. Having one ultimate decision maker does help break the logjam, and having everybody understand it's an open process and there is real input helps people be comfortable that it's not a democracy.

K: How about decisions? Are they directive, participated, democratized, or consensus driven?

R: I would say that decisions are data-driven. We spend a lot of time analyzing. Some things are by decree that are just not important things and therefore we are not going to waste the time going through some issues with everyone. But, yes, it's a very inclusive process. It's not designed to build consensus. It's designed to solicit feedback from everyone.

K: Would you say the organization structure helps the achievement of the goal? Is it designed that way?

R: Yes, I believe the organizational structure does help achieve the goal. The goals include inclusiveness, and the goals are to make better decisions because they reflect the views and input of multiple perspectives and multiple intelligent people.

Building a hedge fund is a bit like building an expansion football team. Some sports coaches say, "This is my system, and I am going to try to get athletes who can do it." Others say, "These are my athletes, and what would be the best system to put around them?" I think we are more of the latter. We have to be involved because we have deficiencies in the system that we haven't yet trained and filled; so we have coaches that are playing some aspects that ideally they wouldn't.

K: You measure performance. Does that tie to what's driving value in the business?

R: Yeah, we measure performance, but in a team approach it's very difficult to measure relative investment performance because who knows who contributed to what successes and what failures? We try to have it be interactive. We try to have it be a long-term basis. We try to communicate a couple of times. We go through the reviews. We give people a chance to give feedback. We try to solicit feedback from others so it's not just my view versus Joe's view. So we make it a more popular discussion so that people can believe there is fairness in the process.

K: Do people have a sense of identity so they feel like they are part of your firm? Would you call it a winning culture?

R: I would say we are in danger of being too friendly of a culture and less winning. That's one of the things we need to dial down a little bit. I am scared that people have gotten too comfortable and forgotten that we all have an unbelievable task to do every day. This isn't about playing acoustic guitar and holding hands and having off-sites. This is about winning in the market. So I would say that objectively our scorecard today is that people don't show up at eight o'clock in the morning with that same killer instinct that I want them to have, and we are working on that. That's a wonderful reminder that we are a business.

K: One good question is, "What dropped out of your strategy?" Invariably, something has dropped out that they may have been doing before. When they get complacent, people tend not to be as conscious of all the little steps.

R: We are spending a lot of time troubleshooting. When you play so defensive it's very difficult to play offense. What is missing are new ideas that are compounding two percent a month. You are somewhat trapped in your existing battles, and tearing the band-aid is very, very difficult. So, we are cognizant of trying to make sure that we don't discourage somebody by saying, "This just doesn't feel right" and, for me, just reducing exposure and saying, "Look, I know we all want to be team oriented, but at the end of the day I am going to chop off part of your position."

K: Do you want the consensus of the whole team?

R: No, we don't want to get consensus of the whole team. We want to get everybody's perspective on how much they like the investment, what they think the risk factors are, and what they think the risk dollars are.

While it is important to communicate with your team in terms of their strengths so that they can naturally take on the functions that are designated for them, behavioral changes ultimately occur as a result of a motivation to change. Therefore, you have to understand the hot buttons and motivating response patterns of people on your team. This may take time to develop, but it is certainly the way to build team unity, one person at a time on an individual and then on a group basis, sharing some things about your sense of their strengths with others in the group so everyone is aware of what each person brings to the table.

Given this, there is value in encouraging PMs to share their ideas with others on the team, especially when they are having difficulty and may be missing something. This is difficult to do at first because people don't like admitting mistakes, but once this becomes a regular routine, where people openly admit that there is more for them to know, you can create a learning culture. In this type of climate, people can help one another expand their repertoire of skills and build stronger relationships with one another.

As the leader it is your task to take your ego out of the equation and encourage this kind of cross-pollination. It also helps not to beat up on people who are not doing well, but to encourage them to do more work and explore more ways of looking at a theme in order to gain greater strength and skill for the longer haul.

To successfully implement this kind of transformative strategy, you need leadership skills capable of calling people to their highest performance. Ask yourself the following questions. Rank yourself as to whether this is an area of strength or weakness for you. If it is an area of weakness, consider specific ways in which you can improve.

- How well do I delegate responsibilities to others who can equally perform the task?
- How well do I assign responsibilities that will help others develop essential skills?
- How well do I give up authority for the benefit of the team?
- How well do I know the strengths and weaknesses of those on my team?
- How much do I incorporate the strengths of others into the work that needs to be accomplished?
- How often do I actively pursue the opinions and ideas of others?
- How often do I encourage the development of risky ideas that I have not initiated?
- Do I reward and recognize the achievements of others?
- Am I careful not to discredit the opinions and ideas of others?
- Do I encourage my team members to set and work toward goals?
- Do I make sure that the goals they set are achievable but will also stretch and motivate them?

- Do I encourage them to periodically review their strategies with me, and do I provide support, encouragement, or guidance as needed?
- Do I make sure that my expectations and the responsibilities of each team member are clearly understood?
- Do I provide a balance of control and freedom that motivates my team while protecting the interests of the whole?
- Do I take the time to regularly coach my team?
- Do I coach in a manner that takes into account the importance of maintaining the person's self-esteem?
- Do I verbally compliment my team?
- Do I know what kind of reinforcements work best for each individual on the team?
- Am I good at pointing out the positive, or do I major on the flaws?
- Do I encourage sharing of information and knowledge among the team?
- Do I make sure that my team is adequately informed in order to succeed?
- Do I demonstrate that I value, trust, and respect each individual on my team?
- Do I take the time to listen to my team? Do I empathize with them, or dismiss their problems as irrelevant?
- How good am I at providing support without taking control?
- How good am I at practicing what I preach?

As a hedge fund leader, you have a variety of responsibilities including creating, managing, motivating, and training a team, but you also have to develop innovative and creative strategies that will give the company an advantage on competitors. However, there is no way one person can perform every needed task within an organization. Because of the wide range of responsibilities it is therefore essential that you learn how to empower the individuals on your team to take on tasks independently.

ENCOURAGING RESPONSIBILITY

There is value in giving team members more responsibility for making selected decisions and holding them accountable for the quality of the decisions. But, while some people are naturally gifted at encouraging others to take responsibility, others have to make a conscious effort to learn how to lead in this way. When a leader fosters the team's natural inclination to double-check everything with the manager, the players don't develop confidence in their own abilities. As one leader so aptly put it, "I would have to be the biggest egomaniac in the world to think that I, with very limited information and limited time, could make a better decision than somebody who is fully immersed in it."

Asher is a leader who has been learning this lesson. Asher is an idea person who is constantly in search of new ways to do things. This love of ideas is a natural fit for what he does since he is positioned where his ideas are valued, and he is able to create and design programs that implement his ideas. He is a very responsible person who has high standards. However, Asher's strong sense of responsibility causes the most problems with his leadership because he tends to overtake the work of the team in an effort to see it completed to his sense of perfection. In addition, he has a distinct inability to relinquish control or build a sense of responsibility among his team, and his sense of focus prevents him from being sensitive to the needs of others because his work takes priority over feelings.

A recent encounter with one of his team members brought the situation to light. After some in-depth conversations, Asher was able to move the dial forward and to empower at least one member of his team to take on a variety of projects that more readily satisfied his natural ability for strategic thinking, his need for achievement, and the goal of aligning his interests with that of company. Asher also introduced the idea of weekly meetings with the team leaders to help avoid further conflicts.

While Asher has always used "the stick" as a motivator, he is now learning to motivate people by paying attention to their specific needs and not assume that, like himself, they function solely in terms of the satisfaction they are getting from their work. He is also learning to manage in terms of the strengths of his players, giving them more specific opportunities to work in terms of their strengths so that they will feel more engaged in the investment process.

Recently, Asher has become more aware of the need to delegate responsibility and to pay a bit more attention to the desire of his team members to participate in the process. In particular, he is consciously splitting up some of his responsibilities with the team. He genuinely derives satisfaction from supporting others but is not fully cognizant of the impact of his focused and deliberate interpersonal style on the emotional responses of others. It will take some time for this pattern to be modified, but he is an eager learner and very dedicated to making this work.

Case Study on the Challenges of Responsibility

While a good leader is central to the communication and decision making of any organizational body, his direction should extend to the members of a team in a way that not only makes himself accessible but encourages communication and accessibility among team members. Sometimes this can be a challenging assignment.

William had been working on improving his management skills and trying to encourage creative competition and increased responsibility when he encountered a situation that he didn't know how to appropriately handle. While William required senior analysts to keep and report on journals and to be prepared to have conversations with him regarding their output of ideas, he didn't readily expect this kind of work from newer and younger analysts. So, he was surprised when a new hire, who had been working under him for only about a month, began writing up ideas and performing various tasks similar to that of the senior analysts. The issue that arose involved other analysts who were feeling threatened by the new hire's behavior. William, while excited about the work being accomplished, was in a quandary on how to handle the negativity generated by it. Listen in as we discuss the issue and other challenges to encouraging responsibility.

William: These two guys started the same day, same room, and one of them is pulling ahead.

Kiev: I understand that, but the other guy doesn't know what he could be doing. You have to show it to him.

W: I like that. "Doug did this; do you want to try your hand at this?" That's what a good manager does.

K: How would he know that's better if you don't show him?

W: Well, he is not only going to know, he is going to be feeling like this is a competition.

K: Well, it's not about how you feel; it's about getting the job done. The more you can empower people to do this kind of work, the more satisfaction they will get, and the greater will be your sense of really taking hold of the leadership role. This raises the standard of work and the expectations of what people can do if they are committed to outsized results. It's about exploring all the ways of engaging people, motivating them, and encouraging them to take risks to find new ways of analyzing companies, building models, doing original and creative research, and getting a handle on the path to getting paid once they have identified a variant view, something that is relevant but is not yet part of consensus thinking about a particular company that you may want to invest in.

W: Everybody tells you what a winning CEO does, but how about the growing pains? Do you think it's all bull, that Jack Welch stuff, celebrate more often and all that stuff?

K: You can't do it in a formulaic way, but I think Welch is spot-on in his recognition of the emotional side of engaging people so that they are motivated to stretch and find new ways of producing outperformance results. This is consistent with the values that he underscored at GE when he was CEO there and that he has written about extensively.

W: We are having a team dinner, the first one since March, and we are doing better than we were six weeks ago. A lot of this P&L is mine. So, what kind of things should I bring up to these people? Should I say, "Good job, everyone; I am really excited about this"? It's very hard for me to do that. I think we could always be doing better.

K: It's a twofold conversation. You could say, "We turned it around. We are up here. We are doing very nicely relative to the world, and I am very pleased with that. Is that enough? No, that's not enough. Because we have a lot of talent here, and we are not realizing our full potential." This is about getting them to tap more of themselves. So, you can praise people but at the same time you have to set the bar a little higher, or you have to be clearer about the vision. There is nothing wrong with saying, "You are doing a good job, but now we want to go beyond that." Don't put it all on yourself. Remember, you also need to listen to them.

W: You are right.

K: To be a good leader, you have to discover what turns them on and what turns them off. Ask yourself how you can get more out of them. Don't forget to get past your own stuff, which gets in the way.

W: Like the way I felt when a young man started writing up Google in his weeklies. I felt like he was trying to take credit for my idea. I thought, "This is interesting. He is the most junior guy. I shouldn't get mad at him for following Google." I don't know why I was feeling competitive, but I felt like he was going to try to claim at the end of the year that he deserved some compensation based on Google because I have asked him to put some numbers together, and that really upset me.

K: If he asks for it, he asks for it. You have to weigh the facts and determine what he is worth to the extent that you're firm. You have a little bit more authority to do that. You can't begrudge people for wanting more. More importantly, you have to be aware of your own inclination and how that takes away and makes you less powerful, clear, or real than you could be. So, when you start seeing how your own attitudes get in the way, you have to notice them. Say, "That's one of those situations where I feel uncomfortable. Now that I know it, let's see how long it bothers me." As you begin to note what is taking place, it will occur less frequently, and the emotions will last shorter periods of time.

W: Right! I don't feel competitive for that long.

K: You can't begin to help encourage your team to get past these kinds of emotions until you have tackled your own. Remember, there's nothing wrong with the feeling; it's just a question of noticing it.

W: And treating him like crap because of it. That's my normal inclination.

K: That is not very inspiring leadership.

W: No, I need to work on that. I don't inspire them to win. I just tell them when they mess up and how they could have done a better job. I have to keep inspiring them to win.

K: You need to say, "Good job. This is the kind of work I think you are smart enough to do. You still need to learn a little bit." Talk to your team. Encourage them to do more. Keep identifying their strengths and encourage them to do work that is consistent with their strengths. A very smart and thorough guy may make a good analyst. Someone who is good at meeting people and has good listening skills may be particularly good at company meetings, in asking good questions and listening and observing for body language clues about what a CEO or CFO might be hinting at in terms of company guidance. He may be able to read between the lines. He may also network very well, while some other more introverted types may be better at building models, doing the math and spreadsheets, and figuring out probabilistic odds of risk and reward on particular investment sets. Your task as leader is to recognize the unique strengths of your team and find ways to encourage them to grow their skills in terms of their greatest strengths so as to build a team of people whose skills complement each other.

W: Good, I will do that.

K: That's very encouraging. You don't have to knock people; you just have to keep setting higher standards.

Your ultimate goal as a good leader is not to do everything yourself but to support, coach, and facilitate your team. You should empower your team to take responsibility for and make decisions about their tasks and jobs, to help them to expand their expertise and professionalism and become even more committed to the joint goals of the team. The more everyone commits to the same result and finds ways of tapping his natural potential, the more satisfactory the results will be and the greater the satisfaction everyone will derive from the effort.

EXPLORING POTENTIAL LEADERS

As I mentioned earlier, successful leaders have a few things in common. They are goal directed, purpose driven, committed to results, and willing to do what it takes to produce the results they are seeking; they are objective and not emotional, resilient and able to recover from failure and disaster, always willing to think through what steps to take to right the ship, and willing to examine what they are doing, to review "game films," and to adapt to changing market conditions and changing staffing conditions. In other words, they are very pragmatic and focused on producing the results.

If you are evaluating a potential candidate for your firm in terms of his leadership potential, you can size up the personality of the candidate and how he handles himself in terms of his level of candor, his genuineness, and his level of conviction about his process, but you can also garner a lot about a person by taking a look at his past experiences.

Case Studies on Finding Potential Leaders

In this interview with Colin, we talk about the importance of such issues in assessing a candidate's leadership potential and in gaining additional perspective on what is needed to develop the trader's edge in terms of leadership issues.

Kiev: What three or four things do you evaluate closely when you hire somebody?

Colin: Just basic fundamental ability or skills. If you are going to start with a basketball team, you want to be good. You have to have some people who can jump and run. We start with that necessary but not sufficient condition. The second thing, where we are different from our peers, is that we run as a team, and we have one portfolio and one portfolio manager. The first few years are hard. So, I want to screen for people who I really think we can make happy for five years.

K: What are some of the ways in which you screen for talent in building your team?

C: We ask ten different questions. We are looking to see if the guy played team sports, was a leader, took jobs that illustrated he has the desire to learn—you know, has done things that broaden his horizon. We are screening for the likeability quotient to the sociability quotient. We need some intellectual honesty. We are screening for work out, which is not at all uniform.

You know there is a kid who has been working since he was fourteen years old. His motivation is that his dad doesn't think he is good enough to make it on Wall Street. I will take that kid, because at eleven o'clock at night he is going to be searching for the answer. When you go back to him, he goes, "Here is the answer to the question." He so definitely wants to be right that he is not going to stand on his original thesis; he just wants to be right. He has something to prove; he has a chip on his shoulder.

K: That sounds really interesting. Are there any other common denominators that you look for?

C: We are also looking for people who have been knocked down a little bit. Abe is a perfect example. He is the number-two guy here. He had a chip on his shoulder. He had a bad career path. He was just kind of unfortunate and unlucky. He went to business school. He worked at JP Morgan three or four years, and emerging markets blew up; he was on the wrong desk. He did a reasonable job in a very difficult market. So he made a bad decision. He made a decision that he thought was going to be right. The market wasn't there. He learned some things on the risk side, and somebody recruited him to go be a number-two guy and start up these venture capital funds. The guy got fourteen billion dollars. Then the guy pulls funding because the thing blew up. So, by now, most of his friends have made a lot of money. He has talent, but he made a couple of bad decisions. Where there is a bad decision, there is a bad outcome. He is the right type, and he has something to prove and ground to make up. He still has the mentality that he comes in early every day. He wants my job, not in a bad way but in a healthy way. That's not going to stop. That's what makes him great. So, finding people with that temperament is our goal.

K: What specific questions do you ask? Do you ask, "Where do you want to be in five years?"

C: That is one of the ones we ask. We ask, "What are three things you expect as a player? How do you judge your own success in five to ten years?" An important one is, "What makes you tick? What's the hardest thing you have ever done?" We are looking for self-awareness. We are looking for somebody who knows himself.

K: A lot of the characteristics you see in people are hardwired. They don't change that much. Try as you might to get people to change, you have to work around these hardwired or built-in tendencies and behavioral patterns. Knowing that some things are unlikely to change increases your tolerance for the differences between people. The more you can see some of those things, the more tolerant you are of their idiosyncrasies and so forth, the more you are going to recognize that we need somebody who can do X, Y, and Z and whether the guy in front of you has what it takes. Is the guy assertive? If the guy isn't assertive, is he sociable? If he is not sociable, is he goal oriented? Is he so goal oriented that he can learn to behave so that he is more sociable even if he doesn't feel it?

> If people understand where they are, they can be motivated to make it work. Maybe a particular guy who doesn't have the requisite skills for a position on his own can team up with somebody who does. The more these kinds of things become part of the conversation, the more people are ready to hear feedback and make adjustments.

Like the two examples Colin cited in the previous discussion, successful leaders seem to be driven by a need for achievement. They are dissatisfied with their jobs and with their lives if they don't experience some form of success on a regular basis. This continual discontentment with the status quo leads to an internal fire that keeps them motivated to do more and be more. In addition, they are lifelong learners. If they don't know something, they want to figure it out. They thrive on challenges and moving from ignorance to efficiency.

As you can see, the trader's edge involves much more than the ability to just direct a team of people, and not everyone is naturally equipped to become a leader. However, many of these skills are learnable if a person is willing to be coached. Let's consider two different traders and take a look at their ability to lead.

Samuel is a competitive risk-taker who is thorough but not overly cautious. He is a results-oriented person who is very empathetic and surprisingly noncompetitive. While he is interested in challenging himself to do better, he is more interested in getting along with others. He is open-minded and a team player. He is very good at listening to others and working to find common ground when there are disagreements. He is a motivated problem-solver who is less self-interested and less dominating than many leaders. However, his desire to accommodate the needs of others sometimes leads him to give his team too much freedom. Because he is not very structured or driven by his ego, he is actually not as dominating as he needs to be. Often he winds up taking responsibility for actions that should be delegated, and while initially empowering, Samuel doesn't follow through to ensure that projects reach completion.

While Samuel seems to be a born leader, he can improve his skills by learning to be more forceful, taking charge, and making more decisions. Some of the ways in which he can begin are to follow through in terms of deadlines, to assert himself more forcefully in providing directions, and to try harder to persuade his team to see his viewpoint. He needs to develop processes to bring people back in line, to hold them accountable, and to periodically review where each player is in his individual tasks.

Ben, on the other hand, is a trader who is being considered for a portfolio manager position. Ben is a smart guy, but he is not a goal-oriented individual. He is disciplined but also inflexible, cautious, and definitely a perfectionist. He is not much of a risk-taker and likes to work from a prescribed plan. When he has a game plan, he is not likely to deviate from it regardless of the outcome. Ben struggles with change and therefore has a problem with decision paralysis when things don't go his way. He is an aggressive person who likes to see results and, as such, is not often concerned by the different opinions of those around him.

Whereas Ben is perfectly capable of relaying orders, he is not very good at following up or tracking the performance of those whom he has directed. In addition, he doesn't take full responsibility for making sure the assignments are completed. Although he likes to serve as an example for others and set the pace, he isn't quick to ask the opinions of his teammates. He is a hard worker who isn't afraid to roll up his sleeves and work alongside colleagues, but he is not particularly relationship oriented and has been known to damage relationships in an effort to get things done. Needless to say, he is not a good motivator or encourager. Given his personality and profile, I believe Ben is wired to be more of an analyst than a portfolio manager.

While he may initially seem to get along well with people, it is a superficial friendliness. He is a skeptic and keeps his guard up and is therefore selective in forming relationships. He is likely to form preconceived opinions that dilute his objectivity, and he doesn't like to have his authority questioned. Therefore, he is likely to be demanding, bossy, and basically unaware of what he has to do to improve things. He will rapidly become annoyed when things don't go his way.

In addition, given Ben's cautious personality, he is likely to stay with the safe solution rather than venturing out to explore new ideas. Although he is good at handling complex issues, he is not flexible when it comes to taking risks or making necessary changes. Given such an aggressive and unsociable personality, he is not likely to be an empowering leader.

*   *   *

Ben is one example of a personality not suited to leadership, but there are obviously many that are. How can you learn to spot the difference? The following subsections offer short summaries of a variety of leaders. Look for the characteristics for success that I have discussed in this chapter as well as throughout this book and familiarize yourself with the wide range of personality types that can be found among leadership personnel.

The "Nice Guy" Chip was a team leader who liked his image of being a "nice guy." As a result, he became so invested in his idea of a partnership that he lost sight of his goal of profitability. He was so determined to get everyone's opinions that he undermined his own role of authority. After much discussion with Chip, I tried to show him that if he were to run his organization in terms of profitability instead of just good fellowship, he might be justified in taking back some of the control and gain back his edge as an investor.

"Job number one has to be to make money," he said.

Job number two is to make money in a way consistent with the values that we hold. I need to trust my instinct when I am right. Sometimes I feel people peering over my shoulder. Therefore, I would rather inertia take over. That's not the right thing to do. It's just hard without any reinforcement from the market even though that's what we are paid to do.

In order to be a successful leader, Chip has to recognize that the reason he had been placed in his position of authority was because his investors believed in his skills and instinct. He needed to understand that the very thing that motivated him to set up a kind of partnership, which was admirable, was also the same thing that was his own vulnerability.

The Intellectual Gavin is a smart, proactive, and independent leader. He is a quick thinker whose desire for instant decision making leads him to be reluctant to accept new ideas. He is a good motivator and has no problem taking risk. His competitive nature creates energy among his team. As a result, he is quite capable of persuading others to buy into his initiatives rather than having to force them or simply issue orders. Unfortunately, however, his dominating personality has led him to neglect appropriate communication skills, and he needs to learn to be more receptive of others in order to improve his leadership ability. Because he doesn't have an innate desire to be liked per se, he is failing to connect with his teammates on an emotional level and failing to initiate collaborative activities in which he can take part. While Gavin has no problem taking risk, he is prone to impulsiveness and needs to analyze situations in more detail, considering alternative approaches, asking more questions, and seeking additional information before making decisions.

Stressed and Skeptical   Devin is a very aggressive, autonomous, and stressed-out leader. His natural skepticism can be perceived as condescending, and thus his relationship with his team is lacking. When he makes an effort to ask people how he can help them or tries to teach them something, his attitude gets in the way, and he comes across as a know-it-all. Once I discussed the issues with him, Devin began working on new ways in which he can learn to be more supportive and to listen more. He also seemed motivated to look at his own behaviors with more objectivity. As a result, he began purposely pursuing relationships among his team.

Since he is naturally a problem-solver, Devin is motivated toward looking for more creative solutions to the problems he is having with his leadership ability. He is working on how to adjust his communication in an effort to offer assistance without coming across as patronizing. In particular, he is concentrating on developing his listening skills and being less probing and challenging, and is recognizing that he has been discouraging people from interacting with him and providing him with the information he needed. He has made the decision to have lunch every day with a different PM or analyst in the firm so as to get to know them better as people and build relationships of trust rather than simply data-gathering; he is learning the value of relationships as the bedrock of building an information network to further develop the functions of his job. To do this he has had to come face-to-face with his natural skepticism about others. Slowly, he has begun to notice an upswing in the amount of data and insights he has been able to gather and the satisfaction he is getting from his relationships throughout the firm.

Devin's intellectual curiosity and responsiveness to new information were key motivators in getting him to shift his proactive, take-charge style to a more thoughtful and active listening style so that he could bond with other analysts and PMs. From this new connectedness it became very easy to initiate exchanges about the detailed analytical work he needed to gather to accomplish his objectives. Moreover, he found this more personally rewarding and less stressful, and he now looks forward to each day as a chance to build relationships, and has become less skeptical about the motives of others and more optimistic about future opportunities.

*   *   *

As can be seen with these examples, when trying to become a more successful leader, often the changes that need to be made result from a slight shift in the expression of a number of already-existing strengths. A slight shift in emphasis can open up entirely new opportunities for creating new ways of being in the world, which can have extraordinary consequences. Self-observation and the willingness to shift into other available personal gears is the key to such powerful personal change.

ENDEAVORING FOR SUCCESS

I can't say how often I have encountered failures in leadership as a result of a reluctance to speak clearly, to set objectives, and to manage the performance and the relevant behavior of people on a team. The general excuse is that people don't listen, and that the PM has spent much of his career learning how to manage positions but not necessarily managing other people. However, I am quick to point out that it is necessary to oversee the work of others and to ensure that everyone is on the same page with objectives, targets, strategies, and the division of labor that is so critical when there is so much work, so little time, and insufficient staff support.

Let me begin with an example. Kyle is a problem-solver. He is motivated by a challenge and enjoys finding solutions. He thrives in environments that are well organized, with clearly defined expectations and established rules and procedures. As a self-assured, focused trader and a thorough and cautious risk-taker, he doesn't seem to be easily thwarted by setbacks. As somewhat of a "control freak," he patiently reviews all his options before making decisions or recommendations in an effort to reach clearly defined and predictable outcomes.

However, Kyle's relationship skills aren't quite as refined. While he is capable of expressing his own expectations and is likely to stand firm regarding his opinions and programs, he is not very interested in the opinions of others or in what they are feeling. He is skeptical of others and keeps his guard up, which causes others to perceive him as aloof. In addition, he is stubborn in his approach to leadership; if members of his team have difficulty learning to do what he wants, he isn't likely to give them a second chance.

Obviously, Kyle needs to work on his interpersonal skills. By taking an interest in the talents of his team members and developing a little more diplomacy in his relations with them, he can encourage them to grow in their roles and become more successful. Instead of just demanding compliance, Kyle needs to learn to communicate more effectively and to develop stronger working relationships that will help build a consensus for his ideas. In an effort to strengthen these kinds of social skills, Kyle would benefit from establishing formal and informal meetings in which he can get to know his colleagues better and foster a team spirit. He needs to seek out the opinions of others, learn to listen more carefully before judging, and consider the ideas and opinions of others more fully.

Unfortunately, even though Kyle's autocratic manner leads to a lot of turnover and the need for constant mediation, he tends to underestimate the impact of his leadership liabilities and how negatively this impacts his team. Even after discussing these insights and recommendations with Kyle, he tends to minimize his need for control and acceptance. While he recognizes the need for cooperation among team members, he is generally not interested in improving the way he works with others. He would rather move on to the next process and project and find people who can manage the team for him.

Basically, some people, like Kyle, are not wired to be as cooperative as they need to be. So, while he is an effective leader from a process viewpoint, he is not that good from an interpersonal viewpoint. He is not an inspiriting leader. While linking his behavior with the bottom line seems to motivate him to some degree of change, without a desire to learn to interact differently, change is not likely to happen on its own. Therefore, Kyle would probably be best in a position in which he manages process and has an assistant who can complement him to handle the softer side of managing others.

CASE STUDY ON A FAILURE TO LEAD

Another example I encountered was in a macro hedge fund where the PM, Robin, a long-term bond trader, was paired up with Chad, a shorter-term currency trader; they were running into problems because they couldn't decide on the appropriate division of labor. The PM wanted to trade a lot and realized that he needed his partner to watch him and keep him honest and keep him from pursuing what he viewed as addictive behavior in his urgent need to get into daily trades where he invariably lost money.

The currency trader for his part was eager to bet on broader macro themes, which basically took him away from the sweet spot he had developed for printing money daily by getting in and out in the course of the same day. What was the solution? They each needed to play to their strengths rather than intrude on the domain of their partner, but this was not something that would happen by itself, and neither partner was inclined to want to have this discussion.

Basically, Robin thought that if they just remained flat they would do fine and that if Chad would just wait until he figured out which way the market was going and then play it on a daily basis they both could mint money, but Chad insisted on playing broader macro themes. The problem for Chad was that the daily trading was not prestigious enough and that he preferred to do the macro theme trading where he was inclined to lose money trading fixed income, which was outside his area of expertise.

Robin was also upset that they weren't making money in commodities, which had been going straight up for the past year. He couldn't understand how commodities were going up, but they missed the run. Robin made 25 percent in 2001 when the Fed was easing. All he had to do was buy. In 2003, when the dollar was going straight down, they made a lot of money by selling the dollar. He was frustrated because commodities were going up and they were missing the trade.

I challenged Robin to lay out his expectations to Chad and try to work out some kind of win-win relationship for the two of them, but Robin was feeling as if he was fighting a losing battle trying to get Chad to tackle those things he was good at and capturing the profitability inherent in trading short term. Robin noted that Chad was wrong the previous week and the market turned around too late to make money, so they got chopped up a bit. That's when he pulled back and stopped trying to manage Chad. At the same time, he was recognizing that he shouldn't trade as much. I asked him how he lost his handle on his strategy.

Robin: Our problem is we stick with losing trades for too long. I really think these core positions are going to make a lot of money. If I can just get Chad to make money in a lot of these trades doing what he is doing, we are going to make twenty percent.

Kiev: I will continue to have that conversation with him. Where do you stop in that dialogue that gets you?

R: I have told him a thousand times: If he could make money it would put a whole new spin on things. If you had a consistent money-maker, then when I saw something really big to do I could be that much bigger as opposed to being down and apt to be afraid of the downside.

K: Do you think he is going to listen to you?

R: He will just not take the positions off the sheet. When we do get a profit, I am doing some guilty monitoring.

K: You have that conversation with him in the morning and then the rest of the day he doesn't hear it?

R: He is like "I am working on it." What more can I do? He starts resenting the fact that I am trying to do all of it.

K: Somebody has to be the quarterback. As long as he is able to do what you ask him to do, however you get him to do it, the deal is the deal. Maybe down the road you want to change the deal if it's not satisfying you. If you are the point guard and you are saying "Shoot!," it's not "Are you going to shoot?" You have to tell him what he has to do and tell him in a way that he hears it. Don't ask him. Say, "Just get out of this because we have got a profit there." Maybe you are holding back because you want him to do his fifty percent of it. It's got to be declarative sentences, not questions.

R: What if he doesn't get out? What he will do is sell this and sell that and move all the positions around. It will have all these mere crosses on six different million-dollar positions. I am like, "What is this?"

K: Does he have an answer?

R: No. I say, "Chad, just clean it up."

K: You have to keep repeating it until he hears it. "This is the strategy; this is what you have to do right now." Maybe at the end of the day or middle of the day you have to look at where your positions are and say, "Look, you have to get out of this and maybe get out of that; maybe you want to add to this—end of story. If you are not going to do it, I am going to do it."

R: Well, he agrees to do it, and if it's not done, I am going to do it.

K: You have to be governed by the result, and since you both are in agreement about the result, however you get there, you get there.

R: I don't know how I am going to get him out of this. I can't keep doing this. It drives me insane. I am tired of bailing us out every year.

K: Whose decision was it that you become partners?

R: Me, basically.

K: Does it work?

R: I am trying to create an infrastructure that accommodates people and that will help me to do my job. Right now, he has got nobody. Look, I think that I kind of know what I want to do in the portfolio. You know, really reducing my trading is a good thing.

K: You are comfortable about the portfolio as you're approaching it. You are cutting back on long trading. The critical variable is Chad. I think you need to be clearer.

R: How much clearer could I be? "Chad, you need to make money trading foreign exchange. Why aren't we making money in commodities? They are going up for a higher year."

K: Try another conversation: "Chad, what's our strategy today in commodities and currency? Where are you? What do you think you are going to do today? Okay, you are here. If it goes up here, take the profit, get out. If it goes down, get out. By the end of the day, these positions all should be clear."

R: I begged him to go home flat, and he won't do it. He likes to have something to trade around.

K: Is there any agreement about the philosophy that you need to take your profits and get out of these trades? Are you willing to agree to that?

R: Yeah.

K: The next step is for you to say, "I know you are kind of addicted to this, and you don't want to go. I was talking to Ari the other day, and he says I have to be the quarterback. I don't have a problem with that. I have seen this before. When you have a team and you have one guy who is holding because of his personality, some of the other guys have to take the lead," and so on.

R: He said something revealing to me. He hates getting out of losing positions. He hates it being his fault.

K: Everybody does, but the counterintuitive, the master trader, gets out of his losing trades because he knows it's too costly to build up those losses.

R: Not only is it too costly; it's too costly from a psychological point. So, he isn't managing the losing trades.

K: It sounds like he needs to be directed. He can't be *asked*. The point is, you need to get him to do what is appropriate. Trust your judgment and say, "This is what you have to do." You have to take on the leadership role.

R: I am well aware of that, and that's what I am going to do.

This is a conversation I have had repeatedly with a number of managers. Unfortunately, many of them are reluctant to take this next set of steps, and in the end, Robin, too, decided he was better off working on his own than being continually frustrated by Chad's inclination to want to trade in a different manner than was mutually beneficial to them both.

In conclusion, I would strongly urge you to go back to the list of questions that appeared earlier in this chapter and consider how you might answer them. What are some of the things that you do naturally? Do you listen, empower others, support them, coach them, and concentrate on their strengths? How are you trying to empower them in terms of tapping into the strengths of the people on your team so that they can contribute more to the team process than they might have imagined they were capable of doing? How many things are you hardwired to do? What are your natural strengths?

What are your weaknesses, and how might you bypass them by teaming up with people who complement your strengths with strengths of their own? If you are not thorough or meticulous as a PM, you may need to have a team of analysts who are very thorough, perhaps even cautious and perfectionist but good at getting and working the data. What are the ways you can expand your natural gifts so as to develop even more in the area of your strengths—perhaps taking more educated bets based on your understanding of a particular sector or group of companies or a particular geography or a particular type of investment instrument?

Throughout this book, I have provided case studies and interviews by way of demonstrating that in the real world the picture of success is a bit foggier than the clear-cut language found in this book. The implementation of these principles takes time, self-examination, review of the "game films," and a tough-minded or ruthless honesty about what is working, what is not working, and how things can be improved. At the core of this process is communication and a willingness to face the facts and to mutually explore with people what are the unspoken issues, the unresolved tensions and attitudes that often interfere with progress and resolution of the emotional underpinnings. Truly successful traders recognize these underpinnings of morale and spend a good portion of their time in dealing with these psychological issues, recognizing that the best performers have learned to recognize the value of a tranquil centering process so as to maintain objectivity in the stressful atmosphere of trading and investing.

 CHAPTER IN REVIEW

1. While leadership is comprised of many variables, all good leaders want to improve, want to win, are committed to their objectives, and are willing to do what it takes to keep improving their performance and that of their team. They seem to be driven by a need for achievement, are lifelong learners, and thrive on challenges and moving from ignorance to efficiency.

2. Not everyone is born with good leadership skills, but many of these skills can be learned if a person is willing to be coached.

3. Leadership is ultimately about defining the vision of your team or organization and giving people the courage to create something that didn't exist before. It means defining the objective, developing a strategy, and empowering the members of your team to reach deeply into themselves to find the wherewithal to produce the results for which you are seeking.

4. To be a successful leader, you must be assertive enough to lead others empathetically without bullying them so that they don't lose their faith in your leadership. You have to understand that others may have insights and abilities beyond the scope of your own knowledge and experience.

5. It is important to communicate with your team in terms of their strengths so that they can naturally take on the functions that are designated for them. Behavioral changes ultimately occur as a result of a motivation to change; therefore, you have to understand how to motivate your team.

6. As a leader, your responsibilities include creating, managing, motivating, and training a team, but you also have to develop innovative and creative strategies that will give your company an advantage over competitors.

7. There is value in giving team members more responsibility for making selected decisions and holding them accountable for the quality of the decisions. The ultimate goal of a good leader is not to do everything yourself but to support, coach, and facilitate your team.

8. Whether you seem to have a "nice guy," "intellectual," or a "stressed and skeptical" personality, you can become a successful leader. Often the changes that need to be made result from a slight shift in the expression of a number of already-existing strengths.

9. The implementation of the principles outlined in this chapter and in this book takes time, self-examination, review of the "game films," and a tough-minded or ruthless honesty about what is working, what is not working, and how things can be improved. At the core of this process is communication and a willingness to face the facts and to mutually explore with people what are the unspoken issues—the unresolved tensions and attitudes.

Index

A
Achievers, 44
Alpha generation, 63
Availability, 4

B
Balance sheet, 109
Bargh, John A., 30
Behavior, 20. *See also* Risk taking
    emotions, 109–110
Behavioral economics, 4
BP. *See* Buying power
Business model, 107–108
Buying power (BP), 61

C
Candidate. *See also* Team players
    finding, 21–26
Case studies
    challenges of responsibility,
        173–176
    comfort levels, 132–134
    communicating effectively,
        111–113
    comparison of traders, 153–155
    creating a culture of change,
        162–169
    creative thinking, 89–91
    emotion of drawdowns, 118–120
    expectational analysis, 100–103
    failure to lead, 184–188
    finding potential leaders, 177–183
    finding the right candidate, 21–26

having a variant perception, 35–42
knowing the business, 95–100
learning to be creative, 82–88
recognizing goal-directedness,
    47–50
satisfaction of creative thinking,
    80–81
self-assessing during drawdowns,
    129–131
setting a goal, 31–35
trading stress, 123–125
Cash flow, 108
Chunking, 97–98
Comfort levels, 131–132
    case study, 132–134
Commodities, 185
Communication
    case study, 111–113
    contrarian view, 87
    with people in the industry,
        34–35
    persuasive trade and, 48
    as a team play, 155–158
Competitiveness, 48, 57–78
    performance and, 71–77
    successful risk management and,
        57–71
    as a team player, 148–149
Confidence, 47
Creativity, 16–17
    case studies, 82–88, 89–91
    variant perception development,
        88–89

Crist, Steven, 3
Culture, case study, 162–169

D
Decisions
    decision-making ability, 126
    separating emotions from,
        117–141
Discipline, 32, 125–128
Down and out, 61
Drawdowns, 69–60, 72
    case studies, 118–120, 129–131
    learning and, 128–129

E
Economic times, 50–54
Emotions, 109–110
    case studies, 118–120
    separating decisions from,
        117–141
    source of fear, 121–123
Encouragement, value, 146
Estimates, 109
Expectational analysis
    case study, 100–103
    definition, 94–95
    model, 96
    psychological dimension, 109–111
Expectational gap, 94

F
Fear
    source of, 121–123
    symptoms, 121
Focus, 53–54
Framing, 4

G
Goals
    assessment, 46
    case studies, 31–35, 35–42, 47–50
    goal-directedness in turbulent
        times, 50–54
    importance of directedness, 29–55

personality factors and
    goal-setting, 42–44
planning, 30–31
recognizing goal-directed
    individuals, 44–47
Goldman Sachs, 11
Gollwitzer, Dr. Peter, 30

H
Hedge fund managers, 8, 15–16, 107,
    168
    interviews with, 8–12, 36–41
Hedge Fund Masters (Kiev), 2

I
Ideas. *See also* Ingenuity
    completion, 106–109
    construction, 88
    evaluation checklist, 92–94
    generation, 74–76
    maturity, 34
    template, 105
    timing, 105–106
    velocity, 105
Income statement, 108
Independent-minded trader, 49
Ingenuity, 79–115. *See also* Ideas
    case studies, 80–81, 82–88, 95–100
    expectational analysis and, 94–95
    questions to consider to raise
        convictions, 103–105
    strategic thinker and, 81–82
Insecurity, 43
Integrity, 167
Interviews
    challenges of responsibility,
        173–176
    comfort levels, 132–134
    communicating effectively,
        111–113
    creating a culture of change,
        162–169
    creative thinking, 89–91
    emotion of drawdowns, 118–120

expectational analysis, 100–103
failure to lead, 184–188
finding potential leaders, 177–183
with hedge fund managers, 8–12,
    36–41
knowing the business, 95–100
learning to be creative, 82–88
satisfaction of creative thinking,
    80–81
self-assessing during drawdowns,
    129–131
trading stress, 123–125
upgrading skills, 110
Investments
decisions about, 12
return on time invested, 41

K
Kahneman, Daniel, 3–4

L
Leadership, 19–20, 161–190. *See also*
    Team players
case studies, 162–169, 177–183
characteristics, 20
empowering culture of change,
    162–171
exploration, 176–183
Leadership (Kiev), 2
Lever Brothers, 7
Long stocks, 63, 124
Luckman, Charles, 7

M
M&A. *See* Mergers and acquisitions
Mergers and acquisitions (M&A), 5,
    14
Merrill Lynch, 11–12
Mispricings, 109
Murray, W. H., 29

N
Net market value (NMV), 51–52, 72
NMV. *See* Net market value

O
Originality, 16–17
Overconfidence, 4

P
Pattern recognition, 109
Pepsodent, 7
Personality profile, 27, 63–71. *See
    also* Risk taking
anxious and insecure risk-taker,
    67–69
goal-setting and, 42–44
leadership and, 180–181
perfectionist risk-taker, 69–71
reserved risk-taker, 6567
stubborn risk-taker, 64–65
P&L, 16, 99
distribution, 63
negative, 122
PMs. *See* Portfolio managers
Portfolio managers (PMs), 7
assessment, 48, 49–50
behavior traits, 47–50
experience, 76
finding the right candidate,
    21–26
focus and, 53–54
goals, 36
job requirements, 21–22
management of portfolios, 37
performance, 71–77
potential candidates, 22–25
review of actions, 52
setbacks and, 52
skill development, 129
successful candidate, 26
tracking performance, 40–41
weaknesses, 48–50
Positionality, 149–150
Probability analysis, 35
Prospect theory, 3–4
Psychological profile, 13–14
expectational analysis and,
    109–111

The Psychology of Action: Linking Cognition and Motivation in Behavior (Gollwitzer and Bargh), 30
The Psychology of Risk (Kiev), 1–2

Q
Quality of work, 32

R
Reg FD, 89–90
Representativeness, 5
Resilience, 17–19
Responsibility, 171–176
  case study, 173–176
Riepe, Mark, 3–4
Risk aversion, 4
Risk management, 32
  experience, 76
  guidelines, 58–71
  successful, 57–71
Risk statistics, 60–63
Risk taking, 15–16, 104. *See also* Behavior; Personality profile
  anxious and insecure risk-taker, 67–69
  calculated, 23
  perfectionist risk-taker, 69–71
  reduction, 118
  reserved risk-trader, 65–67
  stubborn risk-taker, 64–65
Risk tolerance, 23–24

S
Sector, understanding, 33
Self-assessment
  case study, 129–131
  teaching traders, 18–19, 136
Self-awareness, 17–19
  separating emotions and decisions, 117–141
Self-control, 17–19
  teaching traders, 18–19, 136
Self-discipline, 32, 125–128

Self-esteem, 125–128
Short-selling, 81
Stock market, 2
  insiders, 93
  price fluctuations, 33–34
  short-selling, 81
  supply and demand, 91
  technical analysis, 34
  valuation, 92–93
  volatility, 93
Stocks, long, 63, 124
Stress
  case study, 123–125
  management, 136–140
Success
  definition, 7
  history of, 14–15
  principles of, 13–14
  team players and, 183–184

T
Team players, 143–160. *See also* Leadership
  case studies
    on comparison of traders, 153–155
    on failure to lead, 184–188
  characteristics, 144–151
    coachable, 149–151
    competitive, 148–149
    positive and encouraging, 145–148
    responsible, 144–145
  finding complementary players, 151–153
  importance of communication, 155–158
  the intellectual, 181–182
  the "nice guy," 181
  stress and, 182–183
  success and, 183–184
Teamwork, 19–20, 164
Technology stocks, 34
Tension point, 83

Traders, 4
  case study on stress, 123–125
  developing an edge, 139–140
  log of trades, 18–19
  philosophy, 69
  successful, 7, 60, 106, 120
  teaching self-assessment and
    self-control, 18–19
Trading
  principles of success, 8–12
  sizing, 75–76

Trading in the Zone (Kiev), 1
Trading to Win (Kiev), 1
Tversky, Amos, 4

U
U.S. Olympic Committee, 117–118

V
Variant perception, 76–77
  development, 88–89
Von Clausewitz, Karl, 44–45

Printed and bound by CPI Group (UK) Ltd, Croydon, CR0 4YY

16/04/2025

14658510-0001